Post-Pandemic Recovery

Transformational Leadership and Knowledge Management

By Mostafa Sayyadi and Michael J. Provitera

Copyright © May 2021, Dr. Michael Provitera.

All rights reserved. No part of this publication may be reproduced, distributed, or transmitted in any form or by any means, including photocopying, recording, or other electronic or mechanical methods, without the prior written permission of Dr. Michael Provitera, except in the case of brief quotations embodied in critical reviews and certain other noncommercial uses permitted by copyright law.

For permission requests, write to Dr. Michael Provitera @ **docprov@msn.com**, with the subject title addressed "Attention: Permissions Coordinator," and visit **http://docprov.com** for free workbooks, podcasts, and videos.

ISBN: 9798505982181 (Paperback)
ISBN: To Be Announced in November 2021 (E-book)

Library of Congress Control Number: 1796

Any references to historical events, real people, or real places are used fictitiously. Names, characters, and places are products of the author's imagination unless otherwise documented.
Front cover image created by Dr. Michael Provitera
Book designed by Dr. Michael Provitera
Line-by-Line Editing by Dr. Michael Provitera
Printed by Motivational Leadership Training, Inc., in the United States of America. Website: **http://docprov.com/hire-mike.html**
For Management Consulting Contact Dr. Mike at 954-613-3903

Table of Contents

Foreword
Introduction

Chapter 1
From Good Management to Great Leadership

Chapter 2
A Look at Political Leaders and Corporate Leaders

Chapter 3
Leadership Theories and the Organizational Lifecycle

Chapter 4
Effective Leadership Strategy in a Post-Pandemic World

Chapter 5
A Carrot on the Stick Approach to Decoding Transactional Leadership

Chapter 6
A Post-Pandemic Approach to Social Capital

Chapter 7
Transformational Leadership in a Post-Pandemic World

Chapter 8
Post-Pandemic Recipe for Success: Social Capital Coupled with Resilience

Chapter 9
Building Competitive Advantage in the Post-Pandemic

Chapter 10
Sustaining Competitive Advantage in the Knowledge Economy

References

Foreword

I was honored to write this foreword for Dr. Provitera's Post Pandemic Recovery Books. I consider myself an ambitious student. I attend Barry University in Miami, Florida. Pursuing two degrees and I am very involved with leadership groups on campus. Leadership is my passion.

At Barry U, with a great deal of diversity and so many clubs/organizations, there is really a place for everyone. All a student needs are a desire and wherewithal to be willing to succeed, and then, it is imminent. Dr. Provitera's book, *The Post Pandemic Recovery*, written in 2021 but reflecting on the challenging year of 2020, was a highlight of my leadership learning and development. The year 2020, was a one that brought difficulties at scales that no one was truly prepared for with the surge of COVID-19. Schools abruptly closed and switched courses to remote platforms, and this, among other things, came to a surprise for all. At Barry U, Professors and faculty had to strategize on how this could be done without losing the educational excellence that the school is known for since 1940 when it was founded by the Adrian Dominican Sisters. It wasn't easy but it was a relief that some schools at my university had programs strictly online already. This change for other schools really took a village and it placed stress on both students and faculty. Professors questioned if students were truly actively engaged and retaining material as if they were in a classroom setting. As a student, while it was great to save money on commuting, I was not accustomed to learning through a screen and without having any interaction with my other college students, and this stress, added to the challenging year.

As President the chapter of The National Society of Leadership and Success (NSLS). The NSLS is recognized as the largest honor society in the United States. Our program offers students an array of interpersonal skills such as how to work effectively in teams, how to successfully set SMART goals, and how to accomplish all this before graduation so we are ready for life's challenges. Once inducted, members are granted access to an array of benefits that serve as a toolbox for life after graduation. As President, I adjusted my curriculum of the NSLS, the same way that my professors did when they were charged with teaching remotely, on short notice. The NSLS program was brought to campus with an in-person structure, and I had to change that to be online or virtual, in person, or both. When the pandemic hit us, I had to plan for the post-pandemic recovery, I made sure to learn about leadership and what I needed to do to adjust, recruit, create a new executive board of students, lean on advisors, and involve faculty. The Post Pandemic Recovery book helped me to never give up and thrive using transformational leadership and knowledge management. In fall of 2021, I organized the first in person Induction since the fall of 2019. It was the greatest feeling to see members in person and hear their amazing feedback on the program and to see family and friends that are the driving force and support for our NSLS members.

Enough about me, my goal here is to pay a tribute to Dr. Michael Provitera and his writing of this book in a timely manner when it was needed most. Dr. Provitera was present at our spring 2020, NSLS virtual member induction, and he was so easy to speak with and offered our members free workbooks on motivation, leadership, and the post-pandemic recovery. Yes, Dr. Provitera came fully equipped with resources that our students could apply and use for whatever setting they needed. Some students knew Dr. Provitera as a professor while others read his books or attended his motivation and leadership seminars on campus.

Through this, Dr. Provitera and I developed a wonderful friendship, now, and for years to come. Dr. Provitera is resourceful, knowledgeable, and passionate with all the endeavors that he takes on, he is always available to students, and cares deeply about their success. I recommend the two books, Post-Pandemic Recovery, and The Pillars of the Post-Pandemic Knowledge-Driven Economy, to anyone who, like me, had to encounter the challenges of COVID-19, and pivot during this time with resilience and fortitude. The Post-Pandemic Recovery Books will ensure that you or your team are equipped with tools and techniques to learn and apply practical leadership knowledge for a better and more meaningful life, now, and for years to come.

Foreword written by ***Amanda Gonzalez Garcia***

Introduction

Executives today are under a tremendous amount of pressure in the knowledge economy. Stress levels are high, and it has never been so important at the top for CEOs and business owners. During the post-pandemic, leaders began to listen and respond to the plethora of information from articles, books, and models attempting to provide leadership to help impact not only the productivity and profitability of the organization but also the competitive advantage. Even when all the information was laid out and easily grasped by executives, the world spiraled into a pandemic. Leaders realized that facetime in the office setting, while still very important, can be managed remotely. However, even in the knowledge economy, remote work cannot suffice forever.

JPMorgan Chase CEO, Jamie Dimon, argues that the US economy will boom after the pandemic thanks to excess savings, huge deficit spending, a new potential infrastructure bill, and the success of Covid-19 vaccinations (Cheng, 2021, p. 1). Dimon is correct in his assumptions about the future. This brings us to evaluate how we feel psychologically during the post-pandemic. How leaders can help employees adapt and overcome resistance to change, building upon resilience. Questions to ponder during the post-pandemic.

1. **What has influenced your way of thinking during the pandemic? Has your mindset changed?**
   a. *Driving, meeting in person, developing new relationships, etc.*
2. **How do you define your career?**
   a. *Ready to retire, break in new habits, find novel ways of using aptitude, fortitude, and continuously improving, etc.*
3. **Why is the mindset shift affecting your life?**
   a. *Encouraging more diversity, accepting people for who they are, building camaraderie with colleagues, asking how people are doing, respecting life more, etc.*
4. **What type of behavioral shifts have you made?**
   a. *Doing more of what you love, reaching out to colleagues, family, and co-workers, being thankful for each day that you work and live, etc.*
5. **What type of knowledge have you gained or feel that you are lacking based on the pandemic?**
   a. *Loss of conference attendance, lost relationships, new relationships, bonding with cats and dogs, finding friendship through social media, etc.*

This purpose of this book is to inspire leaders to effectively lead their companies. With resilience at the forefront of decision making, the book will help you not only meet goals but also exceed the challenges of today and those that we see as an onset of new technological advances in the post-pandemic. This book is not about measuring aptitude or defining leadership styles. It is about getting the information needed to place success in the right hands of executives worldwide.

With the pandemic unfolding before our eyes in 2020, we found ourselves pinned to Zoom screens and in Team meetings. While technical knowledge was challenged, presentation skills dramatically enhanced the Zoom screen and people stepped up their soft skill approach. "The need for inclusive, soft skills-based education and hiring was apparent long before the pandemic but COVID-19 has greatly accelerated existing trends," (Taylor, 2021). New research shows top soft skills are requested four times more than top hard skills (Tim Taylor, April 2021 @ America Succeeds).

Leadership and Communication Competencies are in the highest demand, requested by 50+ percent of postings

Soft skills will continue to develop as a leading component of interpersonal skill development in the post-pandemic. Research regarding soft skills, like this, by *America Succeeds,* categorized 10 of the most in-demand Durable Skills into 10 major themes or competencies (Taylor, 2021), with leadership and communication rising to the top.

Today's globalized nature of competitiveness is placing more pressure on companies to achieve a high level of efficiency and effectiveness and world class service. Yet, in the face of the pandemic, work falters, projects are stymied, and people jump ship. Retaining talent has been at the forefront of the heart of the post-pandemic and rightsizing will be a continuous involvement of many organizations. There are many academic studies that focus on the organizational and managerial factors that drive organizational competitiveness. Leadership is one such area that plays a critical role and is a strategic prerequisite for business success in today's knowledge economy. Knowledge has become an iterative and elusive process as people strive to keep their jobs, maintain customers, and simply survive. Leadership styles and models have been challenged by various researchers and leadership has still left executives with rudimental and anecdotal ways to lead. This has been profoundly impacted by the pandemic and recover plans are necessary for survival. Prior to the pandemic, the academic literature found a gap between leadership effectiveness, satisfying followers, and meeting customer needs. During the pandemic, this has profoundly increased. Transformational leadership continues to be the in-vogue leadership style for today's knowledge economy and will continue to be as more followers are transformed into great leaders because the demand for leadership has increased as we face economic distress and a global pandemic.

This book blends scholarly concepts with real world application and places a great deal of emphasis on the literature on transformational leadership as a significant indicator for organizational competitiveness. There are several implications for scholars and practitioners found in this book. First, this book adds to a relatively small body of literature and develops our understanding of transformational leadership theory. Second, this book develops a new and dynamic conception of transformational leadership within organizations.

We add to the current literature on transformational leadership by offering novel insights into how transformational leaders affect a firm's knowledge management effectiveness and competitive advantage. This book shows that transformational leaders create competitive advantage through the four leadership aspects of ***idealized influence, individualized consideration, intellectual stimulation, and inspirational motivation.*** This book also suggests new insights that identify transformational leadership as a primary driver of organizational success, which influences a company's social capital. Furthermore, we show that a firm's ability to enhance knowledge management performance, create competitive advantage, and recognize the changes occurring in external environments and responding to them, swiftly and adequately, can be significantly enhanced by transformational leadership. Encouraging a new mindset upon the post-pandemic recovery is necessary for survival but, more importantly, it is the right thing to do. Leadership decision-making not only effects one person but the global economy and all the stakeholders.

Dan Pink, author of "Drive: The Surprising Truth About What Motivates Us," argues that knowledge workers need three things from their leader to be inspired: autonomy, mastery, and purpose. The post-pandemic has brought out two of the three: autonomy as workers are remote and yet still working as a team and purpose as each individual shares knowledge with co-workers to survive. The missing link is mastery, and we propose that transformational leadership coupled with knowledge management is the answer to foster intrinsic motivation, mastery, and resilience.

***

Chapter 1

From Good Management to Great Leadership

The pandemic opened a thought process that reached both forward in the knowledge economy and backward in the dissemination of this knowledge as leaders plan to recover in the post-pandemic world. Leadership has always been at the forefront of management training. However, the four functions of management depict leadership as one of the four. For instance, Henri Fayol has been posited as the forefather of the functions of management. While Fayol had more than four functions of management in his original publication in France which was translated to English in the 1930s. The four that seemed to stand the test of time are *Controlling, Leading, Organizing, and Planning (we coined this as CLOP).* We must add one new word to these four functions of management based on the post pandemic: **_RESILIENCE._** Leadership, being a strong component of management has manifested itself into the forefront of planning and development for many executives and aspiring leaders. Fayol included leadership as a function of management. For example, some scholars feel that leadership was rooted in ancient history. The concept of leadership highly manifested itself in ancient-extended families that constructed clans as the central ingredient of cities found in the Roman Empire. The role of leadership was considerably more centralized at that time, and membership in the clans was highly demanding in order to be successful in what was known as some of our first social institutions.

More recent scholars, for example, Bernard Bass and Ralph Melvin Stogdill (1990), suggested that leadership is rooted in ancient history, and they state that "the study of leadership is an ancient art." One question remains today, **_"Can people be made into leaders, or do they have to be born leaders to be successful?"_** Being a born leader may be an additional attribute of leadership. However, you may be an aspiring leader and, if so, it is important that you develop the necessary confidence and wherewithal to lead effectively. At West Point, a military leadership camp and university, the university officials select the best potential leaders to be trained in the art of leadership. While there may be born leaders among the cadets, there is also a great deal of leadership training and development going on throughout the program.

Ancient writings are rich in leadership. For example, According to Violina Rindova and William Starbuck (1997), some examples of the ancient writings are fruitful. Confucius, a philosopher of ancient China, says, "if a leader behaves as a noble should behave, all goes well even though the leader gives no orders. But if a leader does not behave as a noble leader should behave, then people will not even obey them when the leader gives orders." Thus, in the 1930s when Fayol first coined the application of the management function of leadership, it was not a new phenomenon as it stems from ancient times. As we move through the pandemic forward into the post-pandemic, scholars and practitioners alike must create new models, new theories, and new strategies to recover from COVID-19.

To differentiate the concepts of leadership and management with a pro-consideration for leadership as opposed to management, Warren Bennis (2009) argues that while leaders acquire competencies by embracing education, a manager becomes familiar with managerial activities by undergoing training. This assertion is somewhat dogmatic, however since his position is profound in the Academy of Management circles as he is a well-known scholar, it is worth review. ***However, how is this going to help the post-pandemic?*** Bennis (2009) asserts that the education system is more strategic in nature, synthetic, pragmatic but experimental, flexible yet rigid, active in application, and broad when compared to training principles that manifest themselves in being passive, narrow, and rote. He is not alone. Abraham Zaleznik's (1977) points out that there is a profound difference between leaders and managers. He believes that a leader takes a proactive approach toward more strategic goals and evokes expectations of followers and creates images for them to follow in the direction of influencing and coaching them. He argues that "the net result of this influence is to change the way people think about **what is desirable, what is possible, and what is necessary."**

According to these scholars, leadership is more focused upon challenging the current norms and motivating employees to be more and accomplish more. This turned out to be true in the post-pandemic as leaders emphasized teams working remotely to adapt to new technology and communication tools. Thus followers, now more than ever, considered as intellectual capital, are trained to think about organizational issues in a more innovative and creative manner. Thus, promoting a constant improvement for both themselves and the organization. This intention of constant improvement cannot be achieved without developing trust-based relationships by which human assets could share their knowledge and new ideas with others in an open and supporting environment. Trusting that your organization, your career, your satisfaction, and your customers still exist in the post-pandemic world is a start in the right direction as leaders and managers come together to succeed.

Why is management and leadership so different? A management scholar, at McGill University in Canada, Henry Mintzberg (2009), feels that they are not so different and being a manager is also being a leader. Mintzberg felt that creating leadership, as a separate function of management may be myopic. When speaking with him directly at the Academy of Management, Mintzberg mentioned that it might be a way for universities to repackage a degree and perhaps capitalize on the monetary benefits of expanding leadership programs. Applications of Mintzberg's ideas are fruitful in the wake of the post-pandemic.

A few decades ago, Joseph Rost (1991) conceptualized management as "an authority relationship between at least one manager and one subordinate who coordinates their activities to produce and to sell particular goods or provide some type of service." In lieu of his assumption, management emphasizes more operational objectives rather than investigating strategic goals. Therefore, management has been highlighted as an authority relationship to maintain the status quo through coordinating and controlling subordinate activities. Once the status quo is mentioned, it appears that management is stagnant and overly consuming in nature. It is not, management and leadership are one in the same and to be a good manager a person must also be a good leader and vice versa.

The post-pandemic prepared leaders to deliver communication via the internet and meetings are controlled by networks. These networks cannot differentiate managers from leaders. All people have a platform to communicate which tends to level the playing field. Followers are stepping up as great communicators and there is no room for the shy and timid. Survival leveled the gap between the leader and manager along with their followers. Wide respect for authority figures still exists but the Zoom-type meetings are opening a whole new world in the knowledge economy.

The following table summarizes some distinctions between leadership and management that have been posited by scholars over the past ten years. The table indicates a dichotomy of management and leadership, but anyone can see that being both is much more important than being simply one or the other. Creators of this table are pro-leadership for sure. For example, why would anyone want to **NOT** do things right along with the right things?

Leadership	Management
doing the right things	doing things right
Coaching	Evaluating
taking a proactive approach	taking a reactive approach

having a long-term perspective	having a short-term perspective
enhancing trust	controlling subordinates
Innovating	performing functions
focusing on people	focusing on structure
challenging norms	maintaining the status quo

Chapter 1, Table 1. Comparing the Features of Leadership and Management (adapted from Kotterman, 2006, p. 15)

The table above is of some importance as it is indicative of the mindset of scholars today when comparing leadership and management. The table shows the highlights of leadership versus management with a positive spin on leadership. James MacGregor Burns found that "leadership is one of the most observed and least understood phenomena on earth." Warren Bennis and Burton Nanus (1985) agreed with Burns in that there are "no clear and unequivocal understanding that exists as to what distinguishes leaders from non-leaders." There is no comprehensive definition that encompasses all the leadership aspects mentioned above in table one. Leaders need to keep an open mind and use insight, intelligence, ability, and courage to be authentic leaders (Provitera, 2021). Authentic leadership and management are two important aspects of organizational success in the post-pandemic (see Table 2). The world is counting on transformational leaders, how they use knowledge management to help remote employees excel, help people to remain satisfied, and feel secure in both being safe from Covid-19 and maintaining employment.

Authentic Leadership	Authentic Management
doing things for stakeholders	doing things right for the least among us
Coaching people from the lower levels of the firm	Evaluating people for their best potential
taking a proactive approach to mentorship	taking a reactive approach to problems in society
having a long-term perspective with resilience	having a short-term perspective to control problems
enhancing trust remotely	controlling subordinates by giving them voice
Innovating to save time	performing functions once, correctly
focusing on minoritized individuals and helping them succeed	focusing on a diversified structure of optimization
challenging norms to reduce stereotyping	maintaining the status quo to secure jobs

Chapter 1, Table 2. Comparing the Features of Authentic Leadership and Authentic Management Post-Pandemic

Although the current definitions on the concept of leadership and management are somewhat different in Table 2, these idealized definitions provide various viewpoints about leadership that could positively contribute to define the construct of leadership in the post-pandemic.

Leadership is a combination of influenced interactions and behaviors with groups or dyads of follower(s) to implement changes and achieve determined goals, objectives, and strategic initiatives.

The above definition sounds a lot like management, and it should be because as mentioned earlier, leadership is a function of management. This controversy among academics has taken on a new form. Scholars are experts in management and leadership but very few take pride in being scholars of both.

Based upon the management versus leadership idea, a manager always must be a leader, but a leader does not always have to be a manager. However, with the authentic leadership mindset suggested above in the authentic leader and management table, precedence is encouraged in both areas.

Why Leadership Studies Have Failed?

Leadership, when assessed from a distance, is somewhat elusive. Four scholars that are well known in the Academy of Management, one of the largest leadership and management organizations in the world, by the names of Francis Yammarino, Shelley Dionne, Jae Uk and Fred Dansereau (2005) found some mismatches between theoretical concepts of leadership and empirical investigations and explained that while the theoretical concepts of leadership are extensive, empirical studies could not have sufficiently supported these theoretical concepts. In fact, past studies about leadership lack a multilevel approach, and only focused on downward control. Not accounting for a middle-level leader who takes a two-way approach to influencing both superiors and subordinates. Leaders have become more of liaison between the board of directors and followers. Another reason was that there is no determined set of variables used to investigate effective leadership, owing to the diversity of leadership theories and models with different perspectives about effective leadership. A third reason relates to studies about leadership that lack a systematic approach and stem from interdisciplinary approaches. Thus, leadership has remained relatively silent on how to integrate theories, methods, and concepts from diverse disciplinary domains to provide a rich basis for understanding the true leadership theoretical and applicable concepts.

There is another reason that leadership studies have failed to disclose the nature of filling the leadership gaps between performance and success. In many instances, there is no direct connection between leadership theoretical models and today's changing situations. For example, the world was subtle and nice, and nothing seemed to go wrong. Until a crisis emitted its ugly face in the form of a pandemic. People died. Lives were ruined. Businesses failed. Human resources were now in survival mode along with the C-suite and stakeholders.

In Summary

Companies in general confront challenging situations in which they need to proactively respond to every environmental demand; a comprehensive leadership model can be a basis for understanding and perhaps anticipating these emerging issues. This idea has been reinforced by two scholars in Texas Tech University by the names of John Blair and James Hunt, in 1985, who stated that:

"The issue here is not basic versus applied research, but research that is or is not relevant to current or projected organizational problems."

Leadership theoretical models reflect positivist

philosophy, which manifests itself in exploring the current situation rather than investigating the most desired situation for an organization. Thus, thought processes have changed. Leaders are sitting in the C-Suite at home in the home-office, and for some, it is the kitchen or a walk-in closet.

Working remotely is effective, for the time being, and survival is imminent if leaders take a stronghold of their environments, bend rules with honesty and integrity, take care of their followers, and continue to provide quality products and services. Thus, good managers can be great leaders, and good leaders can be great managers.

***

Chapter 2

A Look at Political Leaders and Corporate Leaders

We fought a good fight, said the republicans when they lost to Joe Biden, who was sworn in as the 46th President of the United States on January 20, 2021. Similar sentiment was echoed when a business leader took the Presidential office named D. Trump as the 45th President of the United States. This notion of winning and losing is what separates the powers of leadership potential. If this scenario teaches us anything, the one thing we learn is that political leaders and corporate leaders are similar.

Where did the notion of separation come from? Well, first, military leaders often provide what is called "Top Cover" flying above their followers to ensure their mission is a success. Submarines travel with pilot ships to guide them. Corporate leaders are exercising top cover now even more as the pandemic awakened them to do just that. Political leaders are reaching across industries and sectors and incorporating more business leaders in their cabinet. The world is changing drastically and both corporate and political leaders are stepping up to the plate. There is virtually very little distinction between the two.

"Can political leaders and corporate leaders lead the same way?" There is vital importance of leadership in both the political and business arena. Success in politics and business can be more effective when leadership is applied to change attitudes and assumptions. Political and corporate leaders can, in fact, make a fundamental change in the processes by which governmental and business organizations serve their clients and constituents. John F. Kennedy's father once taught him about change. He told John that "If it not necessary to change, then it is necessary not to change." This advice echoes through the C-Suite and the White House today as we face the post-pandemic.

Political Leaders are Leading Governmental Organizations

There are various issues and considerations existing in the leadership literature as the core of the criticism (corporations, government agencies, and non-profit organizations) tend to be over-managed (and, in some cases, over-administrated) and under-led (Mills, 2005). Leadership books today will cover the gamut of Shakespeare to Geronimo. Not to say that these authors, leaders, and thinkers, do not have anything good to say about leadership. It is just that the plethora of leadership literature has sent mixed signals to political and corporate leaders. Can all the things in life be mastered by reading Huckleberry Finn? Probably not, but someone may think so.

Some leaders must be politicians to some extent, but a politician does not always have to be a leader. They are servants of Government for the people and with that comes leadership.

In American politics in 2016, a crucial year between the democratic and republican parties, that presidential election has shown that there is a direct connection between politics and CEOs, who at least think they are experienced enough to hold the ultimate leadership position in the world. Political leaders are not any different from organizational businesspeople. More and more businessmen and women are becoming political candidates and the public are responding positively. The reason being---the two do go together. At the heart of leadership are large amounts of followers. Without the support of followers, leaders will fail. The same thing goes with the political candidate that must win the hearts and minds of the followers to get elected.

There are many more followers than there are leaders, and this is more so in the political realm. The question remains: **Can political leaders and corporate leaders lead the same way?** The answer is a resounding "Yes." For example, Eisenhower, one of the former presidents of the United States, in World War II, effectively led both American government and the Allied Forces in Europe in defeating Adolf Hitler, the black-hatted charismatic leader. Hitler has been posited, as a charismatic leader as he converted many brilliant people to follow him but the difference with his leadership style is that he represents the "Black Hat" of leadership. A leadership status that is not only a failing platform but also one that represents destruction as opposed to innovation and expansion. Barring the Adolf Hitler type charismatic leaders, there is hope for leadership at the political level. Winston Churchill, for one. Martin Luther King for two, and the list goes on.

Eisenhower's leadership provides lessons for CEOs in today's organizational challenges. Eisenhower argued that leaders must care for their people as individuals, always remain optimistic, and place themselves with and for the people, and, most importantly, provide the **"WHY"** behind what you ask them to do. Later, the "why" is presented by Steven Sinek, an academic scholar (Provitera, 2020). Sinek mentions that Martin Luther King had a dream not a business plan or goal.

Politics and corporate leadership merged in the past and still merge today. After WWII, some leadership theoretical models, such as those at Ohio State and the University of Michigan, stemmed from research based on military leaders and their followers. This was mostly funded by the GI Bill, also known as the Servicemen's Readjustment Act of 1944, which helped many soldiers pursue academic degrees, participate in scholarly research, and offer advice on leadership strategy. Thus, leadership has a critical role in politics because we elect leaders, not politicians.

Leadership fundamentally affects the way a government performs its functions. Look at the nation's largest health insurer, United Health Care, who out of their due-diligence to shareholders, had to cut out Obama-care exchanges, in April

2016, because they were expected to lose one billion in revenue. Some organizations support governmental policies and vice versa, thus, the two need to be simpatico.

Corporate Leaders and Leading Business Organizations.

Stock investors recognize the importance of leadership in the C-Suite and some investors invest in the leadership of organizations while others follow growth and high relative value in stock ownership. Many investors feel that a good leader can turn a weak business plan into a success, but a poor leader can ruin even the best plan. Some CEOs are known as reorganizers while others are known as creators and innovative. One example of this comes from CEO Rich Teerlink, who dramatically changed Harley-Davidson in the 1980s, and fundamentally built a different organization that still prospers today. The success of leadership at the Harley-Davidson Corporation has stood the test of time. Harley-Davidson's leadership created a more effective organization built upon three primary principles. The principles are:

- focusing on people,
- challenging norms,
- and continuing to fundamentally change (Teerlink & Ozley, 2000).

At Harley, every employee can participate in leadership

decision-making. Leadership decision-making and culture are two primary drivers in the knowledge economy. An example of culture and leadership decision making can be found, in Miami, Florida, USA, at Warren Henry, an expansive car dealership. Warren Henry leaders look for sales leaders with no sales experience but a strong cultural fit with the organization.

Another example of business leaders in a highly competitive environment is Steven Paul Jobs (February 24, 1955, to October 5, 2011); Steven was an American business magnate, which is a wealthy and influential person, especially in business. He was also an investor and media proprietor. Steve built a highly effective organization through taking a change-oriented leadership approach, which highly manifested itself in talent, production, organization, and marketing (Elliot & Simon, 2011). Thus, leadership, being the core of management according to Fayol, as mentioned in chapter one, is crucial to a company's success----both from a performance and management level.

The evidence from these examples suggests that leadership is highly demanding at the corporate level and as a result, the knowledge economy is driven by the C-Suite as though leaders. An example of CEOs as thought leaders driving the knowledge economy is from Vozza, in 2019, with Skyword.

One of the best strategies is to publish articles that position the CEO as a thought leader. This can include industry and business publications, op-eds, or writing on a company blog. Virgin Group founder Richard Branson has a blog where he shares his views and his travels. Paul Block, CEO of Merisant, the company that makes Equal Sweetener, has a blog where he writes about talent management, (Skyword, January 18, 2019).

For organizations to achieve a sustained change and eventually a higher degree of efficiency and effectiveness, selecting a great corporate leader is the key to success. The same with a Governmental official. When the people select a leader to fill the office space of the country leader, everyone looks to that leader to drive thought leadership for that country and perhaps, in many cases, the world itself.

In the absence of leadership, whether governmental or corporate, organizations and countries lose their required direction to achieve a high degree of hypercompetitiveness and cannot implement successful change to adapt with today's global business environment. The post-pandemic will be the final test of surviving organizations and governments. Those that survive the post-pandemic will be the ones that protect their brand, their country, secure people's jobs, and listen intently to customer satisfaction from both a global and local perspective.

As corporate and government leaders attempt to manage people, they find that intellectual capital is at the forefront of success---Bill Gates once mentioned that if he lost his top 50 people that he would not have an organization anymore. Former president Barack Obama has rubbed elbows with some of the most powerful people in the world, and, according to Scipioni (2020), he has seen the good — and the bad — when it comes to leadership. Former President Obama felt that:

> ***...the No. 1 best thing you can do as a leader is to "set a tone in terms of culture as a team." "Whether the team is a basketball team or a business or an administration. What are the values in which you are organizing yourselves? Being clear about what your values are as an organization, that's part of leadership."***

Thus, corporate, and governmental leaders develop organizational communication aimed at providing valuable resources for all organizational members and constituents by building a culture and focusing on the values portrayed both as an organization and as country. Leaders, at both political and non-political levels, enhance knowledge sharing among intellectual capital and stipulate knowledge to be shared around organizations and countries. Sharing the best practices across governments and organizations based on both positive and negative experiences could positively impact some aspects of non-financial performance such as innovation and creativity in the knowledge economy, providing learning and growth opportunities for both constituents and employees.

Empowered followers can enable organizations and governments to actively respond to environmental changes, which can in turn enhance performance. Empowering people during the pandemic has taken a new twist as people secure their jobs and adapt to technology. Knowledge is not only power today but also a way of life in the remote offices of one's home or apartment.

The outcome is resilience, which narrows the gap between success and failure, and this can be achieved by the commitment of organizational and governmental members and facilitated by both political and organizational leaders. When corporate and political leaders show concern for the employee's individual needs, these individuals begin to contribute more commitment and become more inspired to put extra effort into their work. This extra effort improves customer and public satisfaction and impacts shareholder value and voting power. In organizations, this is known as improving operational risk management and in government, it is known as improving infrastructure. For instance, when political leaders show concern for all people across categories, from lower echelons and to the highest societal pinnacle, the people begin to connect more and contribute more to society by helping each other succeed together in solidarity.

In Summary

Political leaders will continue to impact organizations and organizational leaders will continue to impact politics. During the pandemic, barriers have been broken and glass ceilings shattered. The post-pandemic provides a level playing field with knowledge at the forefront of the economy.

***

Chapter 3

Leadership Theories and the Organizational Life cycle

As the post-pandemic unfolds, organizational leaders are managing somewhere on the organizational life cycle. Most organizational life cycle models hold a view that the organizational life cycle is comprised of five stages that can be summarized simply as a **startup**, or in some cases initial public offering, **growth** and expansion, **maturity** and finding new niches, **decline** as competitors move in and steal market share, and **death** in the form of merger, acquisition, chapter eleven, or even closure. An example of the end of the life cycle, **Toys R' Us** found dwindling sales, tough competition, and a smaller market share as competitors like Amazon moved in to steal market share, such competitive pressure eventually had an impact on the company and in September 2017, **Toys R' Us** declared bankruptcy, a smile lost on children's faces as many children and parents are left with great memories.

Leadership theories and organizational life cycles are not researched enough today. There is some indicative information in the academic literature, however.

"Certain relationships between aspects of managerial motivation and firm expansion and growth were found. In addition, the overall level of managerial motivation among the entrepreneurs relative to corporate managers was found to be low, and the previously noted association between an opportunistic entrepreneurial type and growth-oriented firms was confirmed." (Smith and Miner, 1938, p. 186)

Leadership styles and models or theories are lacking a

direct connect when it comes to management implication. Apart from a few leadership models or theories, for instance, transformational leadership, situational leadership, and path-goal theory, which direct leaders to pick a style that is most appropriate for a situation. The post-pandemic caused a shift in adaptability and along these lines, there was a shift in leadership styles as some followers needed to learn new technology and use internet-based platforms to communicate. The question remains:

Where on the organizational life cycle is your place of work and what leadership style(s) are working for your organization?

Questions such as this have multiple answers and many organizations are still positioning themselves on the life cycle with the hope of survival. The one thing the C-Suite acknowledges is that the better the leadership the stronger the recovery from an unprecedented COVID-19 pandemic.

Pre-pandemic, transformational leadership has been resonating in the C-Suite by many executives as a new in vogue leadership model or theory. While one of the authors of this book was an executive at a financial organization in Tampa, Florida, a senior executive asked for the most recent articles on Transformational Leadership. I also asked for the same articles. It just seemed like the right thing to do to learn about the leadership theory or model that everyone is talking about. Many executives mentioned how they "transform" supervisors into leaders or how ordinary people become extraordinary. Another common leadership model, situational leadership, is very common at the supervisory level. This model is somewhat controversial and is still applied to many management and leadership trainings throughout the world. The relevance, while common, has experienced such controversy because the authors went in different directions and yet still use the same name for the model. Blanchard and Hersey could not work together as a team because they parted on the specifics of the model and its application, and they became more practitioner oriented for scholarly review. The dichotomy gets fuzzy when there is a great deal of money and fame built into a model that was first developed for academic circles and then became a training and development tool for organizational development.

Whatever it takes to succeed is the new mantra in the post-pandemic as long as executives are equity conscious, caring, and continuously improving; not only for themselves and the organization they manage, but also developing talented professionals too. Executives are doing what works and if it involves a leadership model or theory, great, if not, that is okay too. The reason for this attitude toward leadership theories and models exists today is because, during the pandemic, rising stars are keeping their jobs and there are more people joining the in-group, as leaders. Most meetings are remote and conducted on technological platforms. Faces are at the forefront and rising stars exist everywhere there is a remote employee. Thus, the post-pandemic calls for transformational leadership coupled with knowledge management, but the collapse of leadership theories is inevitable in a time of crisis. One would feel inclined to find novel new theories and models that are focus on what works but the only thing that works in the post-pandemic is being authentic and understanding that the world has changed, and we all must change with it. As the pros, at the Harvard Business Review say, who often find their novel way into to C-Suite, by leading with a resilient future.

> ***"While the right communication strategy has been critical during the pandemic, it will remain just as critical—if not more so—when we transition back to "normal" (whatever that means). Although we are still living in COVID-19's grip, companies are starting to devise plans to bring their workforces back to the office in the coming weeks and months."*** (Groysberg, Abrahams, and Connolly Baden, 2021)

The statement above can only shed light on leadership theories and process as the office suite begins to populate once again and remote teams remain as a secondary way to communicate. Transformational Leadership has that resonance that some leaders flock to when there is a change process involved. With so many critics of transformational leadership, it is a wonder why leaders request articles and books as reference to leadership models in this area. For example, Lee (2014, p. 17) argued that based on a review of the relevant literature, it is evident that the very concept of transformational leadership is ambiguous. Furthermore, two scholars, Stephen Zaccaro and Zachary Horn (2003), critique the literature of leadership for having no relevance between leadership styles and today's changing business environment. Many leadership models and theories do not factor into the equation a worldwide pandemic or other traumatic events (i.e., 9/11/2001, massive layoffs, or downsizing) and how to lead through these events. Not to say that models and applications may be in the works in research labs and academic circles, but the time is now to find novel ways to proceed in the post-pandemic as organizations and the world face what is called "*unprecedented times*." Some authors posit that transformational leadership style unfolds results in organizations, influencing employee individual interests to align with institutional interests, and through inspiring followers to create new ideas and innovations for effective business outcomes. Thus, if the model is learned and applied then it is relevant to help organizational leaders lead through a crisis. Thus, leaders today, are focused on resilience and recovery and transformational leadership and knowledge management are two approaches that may help them get through the pandemic and succeed in the post-pandemic.

A question for executives today, in the post-pandemic, **_is there a leadership model or theory that incorporates a leadership style that has emerged as more applicable, easier to implement, and more adaptable_**?' Grasping any leadership model will be challenging but selecting the one that works best for the executive will be the best one for them.

Executives are attempting to examine some theories and models that are directed at developing a better understanding of the concept and evolution of leadership thought. There have been several shifts in the study of leadership, and subsequently newer approaches to leadership emerged leading up to the emergence of transformational leadership.

During the pandemic, opportunities may be granted to employees as they step up and communicate to groups in remote meetings and the application of leadership styles and models may have been done without conscious effort. Some folks in meetings do not speak at all or choose to engage in dialogue sparingly. Thus, a more focused leadership development and encouragement strategy to implement leadership through training and development is necessary for remote meetings as we enter the post-pandemic.

How are Leadership Theories and Models used in the Post Pandemic Recovery?

This is not enough information complied to answer this question, as the post-pandemic recovery is still operative. The post pandemic recovery is still in progress as there are increased efforts to bring vaccines to the marketplace. This, on one hand, offers executives light at the end of the tunnel, but, on the other hand, it provides a grey tunnel with a small light. ***Will the world be a better place once everyone is vaccinated?*** Yes. ***Will a vaccinated world help business?*** Yes. ***How?*** While there is not certain evidence answering these questions, we do know that recovery plans are being made. Any talk about new streams of COVID is highly erratic and only causes more stress. While people are complying to the trainings via webinars, people prefer being around people face-to-face.

A Look at Behavioral Leadership Theory for the Post-Pandemic

Behavioral theory has been in the limelight since the pandemic began in 2019. Many people practicing behavior theory find it a subconscious phenomenon. This chapter will shed light on how it works, what is useful about behavior theory, and what is not.

When behavioral theory first came out of the scholarly circles, it could have been the impetus for a change in focus for leadership studies, and there was a strong possibility that it would encourage researchers and practitioners to embark on empirical studies to identify leader behaviors and accompanying strategies for leadership success (Marturano & Gosling, 2008; Pierce & Newstrom, 2008).

It was early 1961 when Ralph Stogdill, Alvin Coons (1957), and Rensis Likert (1961) investigated the behaviors of leaders at both Ohio and Michigan Universities. This was a result of the GI Bill and the influx of military leaders coming to academia with a slew of data and real-world experience. The result was two main factors. People are task oriented and people centric. These studies aimed to portray the best leadership style when delegating tasks to people and groups. Gearing up executives to illustrate the behaviors of effective versus ineffective leaders and how this influences followers. Task behavior tended to be elaborate and tenuous, leaving leaders exhausted at the end of the day while people behavior, sometimes referred to as relationship behavior, led to leaders spending an inordinate time with followers also leading to exhaustion, and, in some cases, frustration due the hand-holding and continuous feedback necessary to complete the work in question. During the post-pandemic, there has been an influx of people not being technologically savvy and, in some cases, lacking the internet resources to efficiently do their job from home. In many cases, it is up to the employee to have a network at home and maintain it. Data support and computer support attempts to support remote workers but, in some cases, some leaders are finding their workers unmotivated and apprehensive to return to work face-to-face.

During the pandemic, when people first quarantined, work was off the charts and people met virtually to save their jobs and stay in business. As businesses were able to stay the status quo and people kept their jobs, tasks and relationships resorted back to normal. The amount of handholding and the comfort level with technology was not widely accepted at first.

Early work in Behavioral Theory began with the Ohio State Studies

One of the great things about the Ohio State studies is that the scholars developed a useful leadership survey. The survey was designed to investigate effective behaviors in leaders. Ralph Stogdill and Alvin Coons (1957) conducted an empirical study in which they employed a Leader Behavior Description Questionnaire (LBDQ) for subordinates to evaluate the behaviors of their leaders. Using 150 items that reflect important functions of a leader, they designed the most useful instrument in both the executive suite and the academic circles. There were two types of leaders. Those that ruled with an iron fist and those that had a mannerism that attracted followers to them. For academic purposes, Ralph Stogdill and Alvin Coons (1957) rated these behaviors using a range between two aspects (***initiating structure and consideration for people)***. Leaders can score high or low on each of these aspects. Those who ruled with an iron-fist were always found initiating structure and those that were magnanimous, were viewed by followers as considerate to people.

Initiating structure refers to the behavior that organizes and defines relationships or roles, and establishes well-defined patterns of organization, channels of communication, and ways of getting the job done. Consideration for people, on the other hand, has been highlighted as the behavior indicative of friendship, mutual trust, respect, and warmth. During post-pandemic, leaders find themselves looking for ques in facial expression and voice tone in followers while subordinates latch onto every word and body language of their leaders and, in many instances, their colleagues too.

After an introspective review, the Ohio Studies revealed two pendulum ideas of initiating structure and consideration for people, Ralph Stogdill and Alvin Coons' (1957) developed four types of leadership styles. These are classified as:

- low initiating structure and low consideration,
- low initiating structure and high consideration,
- high initiating structure and low consideration, and;

- high initiating structure and high consideration.

Conceptually, these four leadership styles resulted from a combination of initiating structure and consideration for people which are on an X/Y chart with initiating structure on the left and consideration for people along the bottom. Based on this chart, transformational leadership approaches were non-existent leaving the behavioral model lacking the necessary application to be useful in large corporations. Pre-pandemic executives wanted to transform followers and simply initiating structure or caring for them was not enough. However, the two dimensions were considered important foundations when leaders determined how to utilize human resources, train people, and guide them. Thus, post-pandemic structures have reverted to initiating structure while having a deep concern for people's safety.

Early Work in the Behavioral Theory with the Michigan University Studies

The 1960s were the cornerstone years for both leadership and motivational studies. Scholars got together to develop a formal leadership structure that executives can embrace. Recently, there have been some new models and theories of leadership and motivation but the ones that were created in the 1960 and 1970s have stood the test of time. For example, Rensis Likert (1961) conducted an empirical study at the University of Michigan, which aimed to define the relationship between leadership behavior, group performance, and processes within a group. This research adopted a mixed method approach and used both survey questionnaire and qualitative interviews to classify effective versus ineffective leaders. This classification highlights several interesting differences in the behaviors of these leaders, and reveals three styles of leadership, which emerge with respect to effective or ineffective leaders. Accordingly, Rensis Likert (1961), the three leadership styles are:

(1) task-oriented, which focuses on planning the work, organizing employees, and technically supporting them to achieve their business goals. These are similar functions to *initiating structure* as identified by the Ohio State Studies;

(2) relationship-oriented behaviour that reflects supportively for subordinates, and is consequently equivalent to **consideration** for people as described by the Ohio State studies, and;

(3) participative behaviour which is reflected by paying attention to both task-oriented and relationship-oriented behaviours, and demonstrating some behavioural aspects such as being supportive,

collaborative, cooperative, and highly oriented toward accomplishing high performance.

This additional idea, participative behaviour, can relate to the post-pandemic executive behaviour and extends the Ohio studies by introducing the solving of both recurring and anticipative problems, and, most importantly, facilitating conflict resolution. The post-pandemic is riddled with confusion of returning to the office and hosting employees at home as new structures emerge. Conflict in and of itself has risen to the forefront of the C-Suite. Stakeholders may feel that the world must go on and return to normal while others are pondering a more precautious front. Vaccines bring to light a whole other debate that has surfaced. We can assume at some point that everyone will have a vaccination of some sought in the post-pandemic. Thus, participative behavior, found in the Texas University studies opened opportunity for new leadership research.

Pre-pandemic, large corporations needed to better apply leadership theory and models and reflected on Harvard Business Review articles, case studies, and academic research. Scholars met the needs of the C-Suite by providing them with prescriptions, models, and applications.

Post-pandemic is reverting to the conflict resolution and solving problems as the turmoil of the pandemic subsides. The new conflicts are found in online zoom meetings coupled with not being able to meet with clients and customers. However, businesses found ways to rise to the occasion and now seek a broader platform of some type of simile to pre-pandemic office space.

Pre-pandemic, without a framework and a reflection on military leadership and scholarly associations, the Ohio State studies, and Michigan State studies did not provide closure for leaders attempting to run corporations in a hypercompetitive global environment. For example, Peter Northouse (2010), a scholar with a leadership book, posits that a leader who practices participative leadership is one who invites others to share in the ways and means of getting things done. This became so prevalent during the post-pandemic as leaders found themselves hosting meetings with the sound of dogs barking and children rambling behind the scenes. They immediately accepted the home office environment and worked to establish a climate that is open to new and diverse opinions electronically and remotely. This type of leader consults with others, obtains their ideas and opinions, and integrates their suggestions into the decisions regarding how the group or organization will proceed. Meetings are hosted with breakout sessions if necessary and new leaders with savvy interpersonal skills rose to the top while the timid, shy, and non-vocal followers became spectators.

According to Rensis Likert (1961), the most effective leaders have a dual concern for task-orientation and relationship-orientation and undertake a participative leadership style to enhance a climate of openness within organizations. Leaders in large organizations began to apply this knowledge and managerial implication were beginning to surface as beneficial and worthwhile. Then, in 2019, the world was shunned by a virus that caused a pandemic and executives fled to corners of home libraries and established home-offices to lead electronically.

In the corridors of universities, scholars challenged these two studies, because of the failure to account for situational variables in order to recommend the best leadership style that can be used for the right situation. There were also the methodological limitations of these studies (Fisher & Edwards, 1988; Bryman, 1992). A scholar by the name of Gary Yukl (2012), explains these limitations in that the selection of behavioral items for a questionnaire is usually influenced by preconceptions about effective leadership or the desire to develop a measure of key behaviors in a leadership theoretical model. He also expressed that the sample of respondents is seldom systematic, and the accuracy of most behavioral questionnaires is seriously reduced by respondent biases and attributions. He criticized this construct of the theory for applying the fundamental assumption of factor analysis, which searches for high association among variables in terms of a similar category. Furthermore, Yukl argues that this basic assumption could be effective for leaders when they only need to take one alternative way among a category of various behaviors. Kind of using a bounded rationality and satisficing to end the search for the optimal choice of actions necessary for high performance and productivity. This became a high concern for executives during the pandemic when electronic communication was limited across time zones as they attempted to schedule meetings and maintain business operations.

While the behavioral perspective adopts a new approach to overcoming the problems of trait theory, the empirical studies themselves suffer from several limitations leaving leaders in large companies salivating for a more congruent and applicable theory or model.

From trait theory to the behavioral perspective, the post pandemic will only survive the turbulent times with a more adaptive leadership approach. Adaptive leadership focuses on the adaptations workers need to make in response to changing environments. This model fits the post pandemic as it stresses the activities of the leader to optimize the work of followers in the contexts in which they find themselves. Adaptive leadership encourages change across multiple levels and adapts to the community in which the remote workers collaborate with colleagues and clients. Who knew that a model, in 1994, would have such a high impact on the post-pandemic?

> *In 1994, adaptive leadership theory emerged out of Ron Heifetz's book Leadership Without Easy Answers. This theory and approach inspired a new wave of thinking in the fields of leadership and organizational studies. A cadre of thinkers joined the efforts to expand the theory's framework and influence in light of its applicability for our unique times*. (Acosta, 2019)

The Situational Leadership Model in the Post-Pandemic

Situational Leadership is a model, not a theory. The academics pulled it apart, finding floors in its logic. However, this is one model that, commercially, has reached the corporate work environment more than any other model created by academic scholars and practitioners. The problem that limited its use in the scholarly arena is that a model is not theoretically grounded in theory. **So What?** As the scholars, say when a new scholar comes up with a novel idea.

Relevance is key and during the post-pandemic, any model that relates to our times in embraced. Situational leadership is one that has been and will continuously be recognized worldwide.

With over 14 million leaders trained, the Situational Leadership® methodology is the most successful and widely adopted leadership model available. Deployed in more than 70% of Fortune 500 companies, our Situational Leadership® Model and influence-focused courses enable leaders to engage in effective performance conversations that build trust, increase productivity and drive behavior change. The Center for Leadership Studies services customers both domestically and internationally through an extensive network comprised of over 200 learning professionals in more than 25 languages. The model, used in 35 countries around the world, was created by Dr. Paul Hersey, and has been around for 50 years now, grounded in Behavioral Science. (http://Situational.com)

Unlike other theories of leadership offered in the past half century, there are three current leadership theories:

- Transformational Leadership Theory by MacGregor Burns in the late 1970s
- Leader-Member Exchange Theory by Dansereau, Graen, and Haga in 1975
- Path-Goal Theory by House, in 1971, and revised in 1996.

How Situational Leadership did not become a theory is simply happenstance. It has good attributes, but the model has not empirically been tested. Therefore, scholars look at it as a passing fancy, a myth, or a schematic diagram that has not been tried and true. Similar to Maslow's Hierarchy of

Needs in the motivational literature. Unfortunately, for the limited scholarly circles that decide upon models and theories, this is simply not true. As noted earlier, millions of managers were trained in situational leadership, and it has advanced into law-enforcement, parenting, and customer service.

Situational leadership was developed to highlight the importance of situational factors and how they impact the effectiveness of leadership. Albert Murphy (1941) argues that leadership is naturally situational, and that the study of leadership calls for a situational approach; this is a fundamentally sociological viewpoint, but not a psychological one. Leaving situational leadership, a tadpole swimming endlessly in a fishbowl year after year (Pink Floyd, Wish You Were Here, September 12, 1975). However, the person being led, the leaders or followers are all part of the mix; this mix is what Pink Floyd refers to as a fishbowl. They are a function of the whole situation (the organization) or a particular situation (a dyad). The tadpole is the leader who turns into a frog and jumps out of the fishbowl leaving his or her colleagues behind to lead in a fishbowl. Followers swim endlessly until the next situation arises, trading heroes for ghosts, and cold comfort for change. Running over the same old ground dealing with the same old fears.

During the pandemic, not only business executives, but also, followers, customers, small businesses, felt like tadpoles left to find a way to swim in a new fishbowl. Either they become self-leaders, or they may swim endlessly in circles. The post-pandemic heated up the pot and more tadpoles became frogs. However, corporations and institutions worldwide still struggle with the fishbowl analogy.

Situational Leadership has been reviewed, diagnosed, updated, extrapolated and it is still being a focal point of leadership training and development today. Henry Sims, Samer Faraj, and Seokhwa Yun (2009), explain this phenomenon as a fundamental idea of situational leadership, they recommend that one type of leadership will be effective in one situation but may be ineffective in other situations. Consequently, this model, unlike behavioral and trait theories, highlights that there is no best single leadership style for all the situations, and conversely encourages leaders to consider the impact that situational variables can have on the effectiveness of a behavior. Thus, the fishbowl remains.

In a more recent critique by Peter Northouse in 2010, situational leadership has both strengths and weaknesses just like other models and theories of leadership. It may appear unfortunate for Paul Hersey and Ken Blanchard, the creators of Situational Leadership but the fact that the model is being continuously reviewed is a positive sign.

Northouse identified the limitations of situational theory. Asserting that situational theory suffers from several weaknesses. First, this theory has been challenged based on the lack of empirical studies to test its hypotheses. Secondly, there exists a high degree of ambiguity that is highly reflected in a failure to theoretically justify the relationships between the variables presented in the models. Moreover, the third criticism relates to the fact that even these models themselves lack a theoretical rationale by which these relationships can be justified. Thus, the studies replicated by subsequent researchers could not have supported the fundamental prescriptions of this model. This model has been criticized because of the failure to account for the critical role of demographics in its prescriptions. For example, old people, young people, high technical people, low technical, the list just never ends.

Some scholars feel that the biggest drawback is that situational leadership may effectively work in dyads, but it may not be as effective in a group with diverse skill levels and an abundance of tasks. Thus, situational leadership failed to sufficiently differentiate between group and one-to-one leadership within organizations, and consequently could not have adequately addressed these concepts. The methods of data gathering generally suffer from bias, particularly in those questionnaires that have been constructed to force respondents to describe leadership style in terms of the specific parameters of situational leadership...rather than in terms of other leadership behaviors (Northouse, 2010). Therefore, critics attacked the model, and Claude Graeff's (1997) argument that the situational approach cannot even represent a theory or a practical model to study leadership was embraced at the Academy of Management. Expanding the fishbowl.

Situational Leadership is evaluated here and now, in the post-pandemic, and barring this sporadic but relevant criticism, situational leadership provides prescriptive and anecdotal applications that leaders and supervisors can grasp. It is straightforward and uses a variety of guidelines for both leaders and followers alike. In a world lacking structure and fortitude, Situational Leadership has prescriptive merit. The strong characteristic of being less micromanaging and more inspiring gives richness to this model. Delegate when you can, initiate structure, when necessary, by effectively diagnosing follower's readiness level for the task. Participate as often as needed and, most importantly, be flexible in leadership style.

Recently, developers of the Situational Leadership model have adapted to the post-pandemic as many leaders are trained online. For example, The Center for Leadership Studies, in Cary, North Carolina offers:

- Situational Leadership®: Building Leaders Online
- Situational Leadership®: Taking Charge Online
- Empowering Situational Leaders™ Online

Programs such as these have adapted to the post-pandemic is several ways. As people feel somewhat disconnected, participants discover the connection in a remote setting to be working to some extent. Leading online is not easy but it is effective if the correct techniques are utilized. By implementing and establishing credibility and building trust in an environment that is undaunted. Situational Leadership will continue to strive in a time where the future is somewhat unknown. Further research regarding the Situational Leadership Model is needed today.

Post-Pandemic Reverts to Serving Followers

Robert Greenleaf, in 1977, became famous in the academic circles for his essay that later became his book title *"The Servant Leader."* The business world embraced the term 'Servant leadership.' Even though, at first, the term caused some controversy in the corporate boardroom. Then the religious clergy spoke up as a key sponsor of the work of Greenleaf, and with this, executives listened.

Greenleaf's work experience at organizations such as

MIT and the influence of Hermann Hesse's book, *Journey to the East,* set him on a path of discovery.

Hesse's story of a youthful pilgrimage that seemingly failed. "Journey to the East" is written from the point of view of a man who becomes a member of "The League," a timeless religious sect whose members include famous fictional and real characters, such as Plato, Mozart, Pythagoras, Paul Klee, and Don Quixote. The interesting point inferred by Hesse is that:

> **The Journey to the East is Hesse's tale of inner pilgrimage, an allegory on human desire for enlightenment and the long road that must be traveled to that ultimate goal.** (Martino Fine Books, 2011)

Thus, a servant leader emerged, and in 1988, Greenleaf posited that:

> **"a great leader has experience as a servant to others, and he felt that this fact is central to his or her greatness. True leadership emerges from those whose primary motivation is a deep desire to help others."**

In some instances, at organizations worldwide, Servant leaders turn the organizational chart upside down, putting the customers at the top.

> ***The world is dramatically changing. In many aspects of life and business, what used to be a universal truth is not valid anymore. Unprecedented circumstances turn the world, and our beliefs around it, upside-down. We are currently experiencing a new disruptive reality, where everything we used to consider as a certainty is under question. The hierarchical business pyramid is one of these – obsolete - certainties. (Labrou, 2020)***

Servant leadership is rooted in the clergy-type leadership perspective in that Christ's leadership when Greenleaf (1988) says that the words "service," "to serve" and "servant" occur over 1300 times in the revised version of the St. James bible. For example, a world leader named Jesus of Nazareth, once said:

> ***"Whoever wants to become great among you must be your servant, and whoever wants to be first must be your slave---just as the Son of Man did not come to be served, but to serve and to place his life as a ransom for many."***

Whether one is a Christian or not, many people feel that Jesus of Nazareth, has changed the way people reflect upon humanity. Religion very rarely reaches the C-Suite because religion is a universal process and businesses attempt to focus on the religious beliefs of all people to meet the needs of a broad group of people. Some executives embrace the concept of spirituality while others look at it as a complex, but important, issue to address in some way. Thus, the servant leadership style highlights Jesus as an ultimate example of a servant leader and suggests applying the leadership insights that Jesus gives us within organizations. The pandemic has highlighted this train of thought as people became concerned for their job and the livelihood it allows. Many people died and many businesses are impacted by the COVID 19 virus. There are no positive things that come from this unprecedented time, however. With safety at the forefront of businesses worldwide, precautions were made, and executives embraced the necessary changes for a safe working environment coupled with financial sustainability. We all can sure feel the emphasis, even tacitly in some cases, as executives plan the future for a secure and stable post-pandemic recovery.

Servant Leadership proposes that only service to others is the pathway to real significance. Michele Lawrence and Larry Spears (2004) in their book, ***Practicing Servant Leadership: Succeeding through Trust, Bravery, and Forgiveness***, concentrate on some of the characteristics of a servant leader, and recommend ten fundamental characteristics that we can reflect upon:

1. Listening with a heart and mind
2. Empathy for all people
3. Healing as a way of staying healthy in mind and heart
4. Awareness of all people throughout the world
5. Persuasion for a better future for all
6. Conceptualization of where we have been in heart/mind
7. Foresight for a better future for all
8. Stewardship by reaching up, down, and across
9. Commitment to the growth of people
10. Building community and solidarity.

These ten tenets can be summarized in the post-pandemic. People have listened intently to the governmental mandates and the Center for Disease Control health information and responded accordingly, whether there was disagreement or not. Empathy has been enacted to the families and friends that were infected with the disease and deep condolences go out to the families of those that died from COVID-19. Healing is an ongoing process today, given the fact that perhaps there is a feeling of healing based upon seclusion and isolation as a result of the pandemic. Awareness of others can save your life if you let it do so as we acknowledge people as life unfolds in the post-pandemic. Persuasion for a better future for all is tantamount as some people are reckless when not following health restrictions and perhaps being what some call unsafe as we experience COVID-19. Foresight and building community and solidarity as executives prepare their organizations to be more resilient in the post-pandemic.

Greenleaf (1988) acknowledges some criticisms about servant leadership theory, and posits that:

> "In a time of crisis, like the leadership crisis we are now in today, if too many potential builders are taken in by a complete absorption with dissecting the wrong and by a zeal for instant perfection, then the movement so many of us want to see will be set back. The danger, perhaps, is to hear the analyst too much and the artist too little."

While Servant Leadership has strong merit for some executives, this leadership style has been challenged for a lack of adequate empirical studies to substantiate its academic rigor and is often shelved as a learning tool as opposed to a leadership application. As an example of this scholarly debate, Deborah Eicher-Catt (2005), argues that the existing literature on servant leadership is criticized for gender bias in its theoretical perspectives.

As executives prepare for post-pandemic, the practicality of servant leadership style has its roots in helping others and providing hope in an environment that seems to be not only hypercompetitive but also elusive for companies to find a stronghold and bounce back from the pandemic. The post-pandemic still today has not unfolded as many organizations are contemplating how to return to office space.

The one thing executives have learned is to be more pragmatic. Chris Lee and Ron Zemke (1995), in their book ***Reflections on leadership: how Robert K. Greenleaf's theory of Servant-leadership influenced today's top management thinkers***, evaluate this leadership style pragmatically, and explain that while servant leadership style is about shifting away from the old paradigm of a hierarchical pyramid-shaped organization, it "ignores accountability and the underlying fundamental aggression of people in the workplace." Leaders should serve their organization and its people to provide the customer and shareholder with the best possible service, but the practicality of the style indicates that servant leadership cannot represent a complete answer to the need for leadership in today's global environment.

Post-pandemic livelihood will embrace Servant Leadership to some extent, with caution, however. Leaders will place more emphasis on compassion and safety for all as the world recovers from the pandemic.

Authentic Leadership Style in a Post-Pandemic World

The origins and foundations of authenticity are rooted in

ancient Greek history. Philosophers are known for moral injunctions such as **'know thyself'** and **'to thine own self be true.'** Julian Treasure, a top-rated international speaker on sound and communication skills, calls being authentic as **"Standing in Your Own Truth."**

Bill George, in 2003, is the prominent scholar on Authentic Leadership who sheds light on authentic leaders as those chief executive officers who:

> *"Recognize their shortcomings and work hard to overcome them. They lead with purpose, meaning and values. They build enduring relationships with people. Others follow them because they know where they stand. They are consistent and self-disciplined. When their principles are tested, they refuse to compromise."*

In the post-pandemic, authentic leaders, truly perceive their own values and beliefs, as they attempt to highly recognize other people as being aware of their own and followers' values, strengths, and weaknesses and this is reflected in electronic meetings. As a result, these leaders are most knowledgeable about themselves and the context in which they lead and accept followers by giving them a voice. In the post-pandemic, authentic leaders will face the true reality of the shift in workplace commonality. They will stand out by leading the pack as new and innovative problem solvers. Why? Because they know their limitations, what they are good at, what their followers are good at, and how they should proceed.

Michael Kernis and Brian Goldman (2006) found that authenticity manifested itself in "authentic functioning of people's discernment of themselves and others. They rely upon four tenets that lead to resilience.

1. Self-understanding of oneself,
2. Openness to objectively recognizing their ontological realities (e.g., evaluating their desirable and undesirable self-aspects),
3. Actions for oneself and toward others, and;
4. Orientation towards interpersonal relationships.

While some leaders strive to be authentic, the C-Suite have bigger challenges to address in the post-pandemic that have surfaced due to the shift to remote work. C–Suite, or C–Level, refers to the C, which stands for Chief (i.e., Chief Executive Officer, Chief Financial Officer, Chief Operating Officer, and Chief Information Officer).

Authentic Leadership, although powerful in and of itself, has received some criticism by scholars. Jackie Ford and

Nancy Harding (2011) maintain that the foundations of authentic leadership are "somewhat vague," and lack of attention to how an authentic leader can adapt to every situation and present different faces to different followers while remaining authentic. They also challenge authentic leadership in terms of its theoretical foundations and approach to adapting people to the collective and argue that this leadership style failed to consider the fact that each person is full of contradictions. Thus, the "*Be Real*" effect of authentic leaders is pertinent but somewhat inflated.

Rita Gardiner (2011), critiques authentic Leadership for the lack of a theoretical rationale by which the essential role of social and historical factors can be justified and posits that "authentic leadership is deeply problematic because it fails to take into account how social and historical circumstances affect a person's ability to be a leader." Being authentic in the post pandemic is warranted but challenging. The circumstances appear to be daunting and expressing sadness, loneliness, or apprehension about being expected to go back to the office is causing anxiety. Addressing these concerns is important and bringing in trainers and professionals is key to an organization's success. Addressing the potential pitfalls of having employees work remotely and possible employee disengagement is necessary. One way to alleviate anxiety is to create a culture of trust and sharing using knowledge management. Executives need to use technology to bridge the "visual" gap by balancing face to face, the use of telephones, coupled with the remote work.

The impact this theory will have in the post-pandemic is unjustifiable at this stage, but we cannot just act like there is nothing wrong and everything is going to be all right. The leaders that master the art of being authentic will remain in the executive seat and those that do not will pander in a world left behind. Being truthful and authentic will help employees bounce back. Leaders need to know what to measure to make sure work is getting done and employees are putting in the time allotted and the hours expected of them. Jim Clawson, an executive trainer, and scholar has executive's measure three key ingredients that provide the benefits of leading people. Jim's recent book on Level Three Leadership published by Business Expert Press, in July 2021, applies leadership to the remote workforce in a very effective and authentic way. He looks at three fundamental clusters of skills and abilities that relate to leading people. They are creating vision through leading people, garnering commitment to that vision through selling your ideas, and monitoring and managing progress toward the realization of that vision (Clawson, 2021, p. 11).

Transformational Leadership: Enhancing Change in the Post Pandemic

Transformational leadership gets followers to be on the same page, with verbiage and motivation, throughout the organization. Rapid changes are inevitable as the worldwide pandemic subsides. People are becoming more technically savvy as they feel more comfortable in their home space. The post-pandemic enlivens a new birth of transformed employees that will feel more comfortable with a future filled with the combined remote and in-office technology. Leaders are becoming social architects as they attempt to consider more of a hyflex mode of operation. A social architect is an executive that masters electronic communication, understands the importance of social media, marketing, public relations, and motivating and leading remotely. Electronic leadership has reinvented the social architect concept as Avolio, Kahai, and Dodge, in 2000, defined e-leadership as:

A social influence process mediated by AIT (advanced information technology) to produce a change in attitudes, feelings, thinking, behavior, and performance with individuals, groups, and organizations.

Social architecture is a kernel worth looking at because it focuses on developing relationships to creating valuable resources. Many executives see organizational performance as an outcome of various factors such as leadership, interactions and communications among divisions and departments, formal policies and rules, and a climate that inspires innovation and creativity within organizations. This makes sense since executives are encouraged to improve the bottom line and increase organizational performance not only for organizational survival but also career survival. Every executive is held to the grindstone of maximizing financial and non-financial measures---their careers are tied to company performance measures. Held to certain standards is the norm and this is not about to change and may even become more prevalent in the post-pandemic. Ben McClure at Investopedia (2021) argues that:

It is hard to read the business news without coming across reports about the salaries, bonuses, and stock option packages awarded to chief executives of publicly traded companies. Making sense of the numbers to assess how companies are paying their top brass is not easy. Investors must ensure that executive compensation is working in their favor.

While financial success leads to succession planning and resilience, it does not mention the concept of becoming social architects. Social capital may be put on hold as organizations become settled in the post-pandemic, but flexible work arrangements will still hold value.

Not long ago, Bill Gates shared what he thinks is the most important perk companies can give the best employees: flexible work arrangements. Now a new study from Harvard Business School says companies that let their employees "work from anywhere" and work whenever they want wind up with employees who are more loyal, more productive, and cost less. (Murphy, 2019, p. 1)

The problem lies between emphasizing the stockholder's best interest before the employees and, at times, before the customers. The post-pandemic is revealing that flexible work schedules may be the way of the future. Thus, social architects may be able to increase organizational performance and help close the gap between success and possible failure.

Resilience, still being the cornerstone of the post-pandemic as executives master what it takes to succeed. The formula for success is to use Transformational Leadership to contribute to organizational performance through developing relationships with subordinates that link follower's individual interests to the organization's collective interests. Executives can use transformational leadership to impact various aspects of financial and non-financial performance (García-Morales, Jiménez-Barrionuevo & Gutiérrez-Gutiérrez, 2012; Patiar & Mia, 2009; Zhu, Chew & Spangler, 2005). Look at Table 1.

Transformational Leadership Style Encapsulated

Four Dimensions	Financial	Non-Financial
Idealized Influence	Higher Stocks	Personal Attention
Individual Consideration	Wealth	Coaching
Inspirational Motivation	Self-Value	Well Rounded
Intellectual Stimulation	Knowledge	Think-tank

Table 1. Effects of Transformational Style on Financial and Non-Financial Performance

In 2005, Kwang Yoon divided intellectual capital into four categories:

1. Human capital
2. Customer capital
3. Organizational capital, and;
4. Intellectual capital.

Yoon (2005) argues that in order to generate value from intellectual capital, organizations need to manage knowledge flows between human capital, customer capital, organizational capital, and intellectual capital. In the wake of the post-pandemic, human capital is at the forefront followed by the technology to communicate. Customer capital is so important as people are finding new and improved ways of purchasing items while loyalty is fleeting to the best provider. Organizational capital is built upon a brand and customers are relying on that brand to deliver in a time of uncertainty. Intellectual capital has the capacity to leave the competition behind and build a strong strategic initiative by infusing talent prepared for survival. Knowledge, in the form of intellectual capital, is a significant indicator of improving organizational performance as the adage goes "Knowledge is Power!"

The post-pandemic places leadership in a new perspective as executives understand the leadership styles that they use electronically. Transformational leadership, which is not too much different from authentic leadership, places more emphasis on applying what works best for them in their current work environment. With a slew of academic and leadership writers vying for room in C-Suite, selective attention to the best model and theory becomes elusive. Some models may far exceed theoretical concepts if the leader embraces and disseminates it well and in an advocating manner. With newer approaches to leadership, emerging on a daily basis, what is to come of executive choice. One fact is they better select some model or theory of leadership and implement it to win the race of success in a post-pandemic world.

In Summary

The heart of Transformational Leadership is motivating people to do more and be more than they would be naturally. "Transformational leadership allows workers to feel connected to their organization. Transformational leaders motivate by increasing self-efficacy in followers, by facilitating social identification within a group, and by linking organizational values to follower values," (Lynch, 2016).

Coupled with the knowledge-based economy, transformational leadership style represents an effective way to develop and manage intellectual capital. With remote work, there may be wider spans of control and this leadership style influences the span of control. Thus, wider spans of control will necessitate leaders that are more transformational. Globally, business environments involve a high level of uncertainty; organizations will increasingly need more transformational leaders to be more effective.

By focusing on the soft skills, the transformational leader can help organizations compete in the post pandemic.

Over and over again, organizational leaders say that while colleges do a great job providing technical training and knowledge to their students, which is not what they need most from higher education. Indeed, many companies increasingly believe they can

> *provide much of that content themselves. Where they really struggle is finding — or developing — workers with the uniquely human skills that make for a great employee. (Thompson, 2021, p. 1)*

Competition is massive and only a few organizations in each industry will survive. There will be mergers, acquisitions, and the organizational life cycle will be impacted due to the post-pandemic. Historians and academics have observed that organizations, like living organisms, have life cycles. They are born (established or formed), they grow and develop, they reach maturity, they begin to decline and age, and finally, in many cases, they die.

Studies of the organizational life cycle (OLC) has resulted in various predictive models. These models are linked to the study of organizational growth and development. Organizations at any stage of the life cycle are impacted by external environmental circumstances as well as internal factors. We are all aware of the rise and fall of organizations and entire industries. The key is to manifest the capacity to survive and prosper and building upon knowledge management coupled with transformational leadership will help organizations recover.

***

Chapter 4

Effective Leadership Strategy in the Post-Pandemic World

Global strategy is introduced once again, this time as a pandemic that surpasses our beliefs of safety and security. Each country, each city, each organization has implemented some effort to eradicate the possibility of COVID-19. The C-Suite is spending more time on how to lead during this crisis and less time on why we need to. We place a new emphasis on transformational leadership strategy, not only because of the transformative nature of the model, but also, because of its ease of implementation by managers at all organizational levels.

This chapter shows how transformational leadership can be an ideal leadership strategy in enabling organizations to build knowledge-based organizations that create and implement innovations timely as they operate and compete in the global marketplace.

Implementing Transformational Leadership Strategy

Chien, in 2001 presented executives with a correlation between leadership effectiveness of different leadership strategies adopted by executives in internationally operating companies. Global leaders, in Taiwan, at the highest levels adopted transformational leadership strategy. Makes sense since Bruce Avolio, David Waldman, and Francis Yammarino, in 1991, illustrated that transformational leadership strategy plays a crucial role in developing a learning climate in organizations. Avolio's team of scholars argued that Transformational Leadership, by individualizing consideration of follower's needs and subsequently empowering them to pursue organizational goals, they accomplished more. Enabling companies to respond to changes in the external environment, creating sustainable change. The post-pandemic has developed a new mindset a systemic change in the way we operate organizations. Work today is highly dependent on stimulating continuous learning within organizations through internet meetings and webinars developed to train and develop both new and seasoned employees. Thus, sustainable change impacts post-pandemic efforts of recovery as organizations re-size, innovate, create, and bounce back from the repercussion with resilience.

Resilience brings to light selecting and implementing a leadership strategy that goes beyond operational risk management and profitability. It is a survival tactic. Transformational leadership, with its easily adoptable and applicable leadership strategy cannot only help organizations bounce back in a productive and profitable way but also add to competitive advantage. For example, Transformational leadership positively impacts an organization's effectiveness of leadership in building learning through facilitating knowledge sharing by all leaders and followers of the organization. Since knowledge is carried over wires, phones, and technological platforms, executives require people who are engaged and inspired to meet the demands of day-to-day operations.

When a leadership model is accepted, any model for that matter, executives are able to answer the questions necessary to apply leadership without having to delve through all the leadership strategies to find what works well for them and what does not. The model of leadership has to help leaders provide effectiveness and efficiency of leadership in global environments. This is done by establishing commitment, flexibility, and innovation as necessary attributes for success of companies in the global era (Kasul & Motwani, 1995).

The global era represents cross-cultural settings and requires executives who can adapt to various environments successfully. The major tasks of leaders in the global era include empowering employees, generating a shared vision, and creating fundamental changes at the organizational level. This changed drastically as the climate of efficiency and effectiveness was challenged by time zones and governmental regulation to keep people safe from the effects of COVID-19.

Sustained performance in the global era is dependent on continuous learning as the post-pandemic places pressure on executives to become more resilient. If used correctly, transformational leaders may be able to build a learning workplace through empowering employees. They can improve knowledge sharing and enhance organization performance through empowering human resources and enabling organizational change.

Change is more rapid then ever as we enter the post-pandemic. While all organizations are changing, there are stopgaps and strongholds that are trying to limit the change to a more acceptable approach. Second to resilience, is the word bouncing off the walls of the C-Suite, is adaptability.

> ***"It is not the most intellectual of the species that survives; it is not the strongest that survives; but the species that survives is the one that is able to adapt to and to adjust best to the changing environment in which it finds itself." (Charles Darwin in his "Origin of Species)***

Adaptive leadership holds true today as executives are grasping at straws of hope. The model of adaptive leadership provides the impetus for success. Executives are dealing with situational challenges and adapting the workflow accordingly. Giving followers a voice is valuable in the global era because employee's attitudes and values in implementing change are important for success. Enabling performance through implementing organizational change and developing a shared vision for future expansion or, in today's turbulent economy, survival of business operations, a new mantra or global mindset.

The post-pandemic has brought new light to organizational innovation, which can be defined, by Fariborz Damanpour (1991), as ***innovative products or services introduced to meet an external user market need or enhance an existing one***. Executive's today must demonstrate and facilitate the generation of new ideas and motivate employees to approach organizational problems in a more novel way. Giving the work back to people that run the day-to-day operations for a more decentralized flatter organization with organic teamwork. Always, asking for input at all levels, including the front lines.

Creating an organizational vision is the cornerstone of previous success and ingenuity propagated into the future. However, the post-pandemic changed all that. Past success may be irrelevant as new needs and desires of consumers have changed. Sure, old money, saved reserves will prevail but for how long?

As the COVID-19 crisis subsides, transformational leaders have been posited to be visionary leaders that attempt to develop a shared and inspiring vision for the future.

The COVID-19 pandemic seems only to have accelerated the need for this transformation. In order to survive, thrive, and compete successfully, companies now have only two years (or less) to get to where they might otherwise have hoped to be in five. **(Dosik, Bhalla, and Bailey, 2020)**

Leaders play a critical role in shifting organizations toward the creation of new services and products, which is a necessary corollary in a chaotic and turbulent environment.

Organizations need to meet dynamic market needs as technology drives the market and new communication tools are utilized. New and strategic opportunities are harnessed to meet the needs of customers in the emerging marketplace. The executives that can be most creative, most innovative, and most rewarding to stakeholders, will survive.

Organizational innovation is somewhat underutilized in organizations worldwide today due to the worldwide pandemic, except for the newly surfaced meeting software. There is a direct correlation between post-pandemic success and organizational innovation. Many scholars, such as Dong Jung, Chee Chow, and Anne Wu, in 2003, highlighted transformational leadership strategy as an enabler of innovation. Transformational leadership strategy, which has been posited as a managerial-based competency for organizations, may improve organizational performance, enhance the degree of resilience, and challenge the ever-arching operational risk management issues faced today. Transformational leadership strategy, when effectively implemented, may change attitudes and assumptions at the individual level, creating collective interests for cultural adaptation. The key is to secure and sustain a foothold in the ever-expansive global marketplace.

Managerial Implications

In 1995, an Industry Task Force on Leadership and Management Skills found relevant information that may help leaders embrace transformational leadership in the post-pandemic. The task force first critiqued top managers and found them to be inadequate and ineffective leaders. The report illustrates the weaknesses in leaders as **failing to develop a clear vision** for the future of their organization. More recently, a comprehensive study of top managers, globally, in the manufacturing sector scored the least in the very important organizational behavior tenet of **people management** when compared to two other areas of operations and performance management. Harvard Busines School scholars, (Nicholas Bloom, Christos Genakos, Raffaella Sadun, and John Van Reenen) found two salient points worth noting:

Point one, "Among private-sector firms, those owned and run by the founders or their descendants, especially firstborn sons, tend to be badly managed as compared to firms with professional (external, nonfamily)." And **point two**, "The level of education of both managers and nonmanagers is strongly linked to better management practices."

These findings are indicative of the need for organizations to focus on human assets in order to achieve sustained competitiveness.

Due to the traumatic impact of the pandemic, scholars recommend that companies must improve their human resource related practices with a target of attracting, retaining, and promoting their human resources so that they can better deal with the shift in the workforce from office space to home, or some form of both----a hybrid model.

Focusing on developing a new or temporary strategic vision for their future strategic initiatives and organizational innovation necessary to carry them through the post-pandemic. By accepting the challenge of innovation, developing human resources, and a transformational leadership strategy, executives may overcome their deficiencies and lead better in our hypercompetitive environment.

In Summary

Executives in international companies can now take new initiatives necessary to band together to address post-pandemic issues and hone managerial decision-making by coming up with viable solutions for success. Together, in solidarity, practicing managers can accept and understand the importance of the behavioral processes and grasp the fact that employees are valuable resources rather than simple tools used as a function of running a business.

Transformational leadership strategy influences the span of control that leaders possess; it influences the collaboration with all levels of the organization, including government relations, and universities, to make the world a safe and productive place. Thus, to avoid entropy, and to remain competitive, sustainable, efficient, effective, and safe, effective leadership strategy is essential for business growth and prosperity in the global business arena.

***

Chapter 5

Transactional Leadership: A Carrot on the Stick Approach

*T*ransactional leadership is not the best leadership style and should not be used over a long period of time. It is useful when a leader is addressing a project or new employee, or when first teaching something that is detailed and needs clarification. With the post-pandemic, transactional leadership has been positioned to help the masses with the new technology and meeting platforms.

Decoding Transactional Leadership Style

Transactional leadership means just what it says. It is a quid per quo type of relationship between the follower and leader. A carrot on the stick approach. It involves determining the tasks, rewarding goal achievement, and punishing failure when goals are not attained. Two scholars by the names of Antonio Marturano and Jonathan Gosling, in 2008, believe that the effectiveness of this leadership style is dependent on two conditions. One being that the current differences in organizational hierarchies and structures are accepted by subordinates, and the second, being that all the employees are able to work toward mutual exchange of benefits where they are rewarded for achieving the determined goals.

There is a reactive component to transactional leadership, and in some cases, it is a passive-aggressive approach. A benefit or reward can be held back or taken away if the follower did not achieve the determined goals. Rewards are the carrots on the stick and are used to motivate followers and this makes transactional leadership an attractive leadership style.

Transactional leadership assumes impersonal interactions where leaders do not consider higher humanistic desires or relationships between leaders and followers. While it has its limitations, it is still widely used in organizations. The sources of power by French and Raven, in 1959, who focused on people with titles having *legitimate* power to influence followers. Some leaders use coercive power to threaten followers. Most predominantly, **reward** power is used in transactional leadership as a quid pro quo relationship. **Expertise** and **referent** power can be exerted as "I have the experience, knowledge, and education, and you do not," or refer to me as your leader for decision-making and as a role model of leadership.

In the post pandemic, transactional leadership is used to corral as people move back into the office or some version of that becomes apparent. Some people need to be nudged, coerced, and motivated. Some scholars, such as James MacGregor Burns (1978), Edwin Hollander (1984) and Arthur Jue (2004) illustrate that transactional leadership is successful in developing mutual exchange between leaders and employees in organizations. The fact that it is effective in attaining goals is the reason that it is so popular among practicing managers today. Leaders can use this style of leadership sparingly, only on occasion, when new details and tasks are assigned.

Another aspect of the transactional style is passive management by exception or laissez-faire leadership. Laissez-faire is characterized through managing the situation where a problem has occurred, and leaders take a reactive approach to correct mistakes or to overcome problems. This was uncovered by Blake and Mouton in the management grid research and still has importance in clarifying the type of transactional leader in some instances. Some people prefer a passive leader that gives them a chance to use their own skills to complete tasks while others look for leaders that are most present in situations. In the post-pandemic world, leaders have remained on the same playing field as followers as the virtual meetings cannot justify a difference when speaking. Authority still holds and respect enamored but the field has become leveled in the way of communication making transactional leadership more profound.

Critics exist and it is proposed that this leadership style is not concerned with proactively identifying or preventing problems. They do not advocate for knowledge sharing and joint problem solving with subordinates. Hence, it is rational to state that laissez-faire leaders do not possess high commitment in seeking the proposed solutions jointly with their subordinates. Moreover, when such leaders assume the responsibility or intervention to solve problems, they rarely consider the empowerment of their employees to assist. Post-pandemic is a wait and listen and then respond situation today as followers await decision-making and the "*Hallway Highway*" remains the norm. Remote workers not only wait for communication to abound but also have a sense of loss that they may miss out on communication or not get it fast enough from executives. The question remains. *How much communication is good communication in a post-*

pandemic world?

One answer comes in the form of empowering people, which is not new. A scholar by the name of Josef Frischer (2006), suggested that leaders today should empower followers to engage in problem solving. In this way, transactional leadership can be used to review tasks, goals, and requirements of subordinates but then move to more empowerment type leadership style. This happens to be a moving target in the post-pandemic world.

Decoding Transactional Leadership Practices

Executives are bombarded today from magazines, journals, newspapers, pamphlets, news wires, press releases, and talking heads that it is not uncommon to keep the status quo and focus on day-to-day operations. With all these new in vogue leadership theories and models that attempt to consider leadership as an enabler of firm performance, there is an increased emphasis on the important role of leaders when interacting with followers and stakeholders (Anderson & The American Productivity & Quality Centre, 1996).

James MacGregor Burns (1978) posited transactional leadership theory, as a new performance paradigm evident in organizations today. He found that transactional leaders play an important role in improving organizational performance.

Burns was well known at the time and both scholars and practicing professionals listened to him. Understanding the dimensions of transactional leadership and how they relate to follower performance provides a significant realization that executives need to control their environments. Thus, many leaders throughout the organization are involved in determining tasks, rewarding goal achievement, and, if necessary, punishing failure in attaining goals. Sadly, for many leaders, transactional leadership style is their primary way of influencing followers.

Decoding transactional leadership is dependent upon two conditions. One, by **synthesizing,** Antonio Marturano and Jonathan Gosling, in 2008, identified a way to decode transactional leadership. The effectiveness of transactional leadership style is dependent on culturally accepting structure of current differences in organizational hierarchies. Two, all the employees are able to work toward mutual exchange of benefits and are rewarded for achieving the determined goals. This works in the financial sector in which employees go on what is called a bonus-run in which they identify what they accomplished and how their goals and objectives could get them a higher bonus. It is an apparent run for a bonus filled with aggression coupled with assertiveness.

Scholars look at transactional leadership as a myth, or a schematic diagram that has not been tested and verified. On the other hand, some executives agree and feel that centralizing all decision-making and tall structures are necessary in any work environment.

The myth of transactional leadership, therefore, consists between what James MacGregor Burns (1978) and Edwin Hollander (1984) illustrate as transactional leadership being useful in developing mutual exchange between leaders and employees in organizations. Although, there is some fallacy with the myth in that it can be inferred that transactional leadership is linked with organizational performance, particularly in terms of achieving goals, there is no sustainable impact that can be determined when using transactional leadership. Thus, it may work in the short run, but long-term leadership effectiveness is dependent upon a variation of styles of leadership.

The second myth of transactional leadership is based upon the usefulness of transactional leadership. For instance, transactional leadership style has been critiqued by scholars as a leadership approach that is not concerned with proactively identifying or preventing problems. This is a myth because transactional leaders do advocate for knowledge sharing and joint problem solving with subordinates but if all is going well, perhaps any leadership style appears to be working well. Only in chaos, profitability concerns, and turbulent environments is leadership style challenged. In the corporate world, challenge may come in the form of acquisitions, mergers, or letting go of the C-Suite leaders.

Finally, in the post-pandemic, the myth of transactional leadership further delineates the suggestion that leaders today should empower followers to engage in problem solving. Leaders are using transactional leadership to set goals and determine tasks and then, when time allows, move toward more transformational leadership, and place more emphasis on empowering and engaging followers. Transactional leadership can be found in the resistance of workers' reluctance to return to the office in the post-pandemic.

In Summary

While transactional leadership has been through the dark ages of leadership circles, it still has some merit in the short term and is a useful leadership style. There are four scholars, Timothy Obiwuru, Andy Okwu, Victoria Akpa, and Idowu Nwankwere, which in 2011, affirm that the critical role of transactional leaders in enhancing non-financial performance, particularly in terms of improving organizational commitment, may have merit. However, Transactional leadership does not provide a frank appellation of importance when beginning a leader-follower relationship, when downsizing, when upsizing, when onboarding, and when making significant changes to the structure and organizational improvement. It appears to be coercive in nature even in the short run and should be used with caution.

***

Chapter 6

A Post-Pandemic Approach to Social Capital

Building social capital in organizations throughout the world is the primary concern for executives as they meet electronically. The word in and of itself gives the indication of socializing. However, with the post-pandemic it may be unyielding. Many people like working electronically in the remote setting but the biggest drawback is the lack of socialization, and this is one of the primary reasons that workers will return to the office in some remote hybrid mode.

The question is **why is social capital so important?** Social Capital is influenced by the leader. Ed Schein (2016) found that: "If the employees are not doing something that they should be doing, the leader can provide support for the team. If the employees succeed, then that behavior is justified with the appropriate beliefs and values." Building social capital is valuable to any organization as people feel as if their work is secure and the workplace is like an extended family. Social Capital is the resource that keeps the culture together and builds upon the foundation that helps organizations and companies prosper. Social capital influences employee relationships and helps people create new ideas and innovations.

Executives can build social capital, manage, and create competitive advantage. In 1977, Pierre Bourdieu coined the term '*social capital.*' We are human beings and for many positions, we cannot be replaced by machinery, when executives' pay attention to not only feelings of employees, but also those of others, they look out for the follower's wellbeing. This builds social capital.

Social capital originally came from earlier concepts associated with social and economic sciences (such as social capability and civic virtue), and to some extent is driven from political theorists (such as Alexis de Tocqueville and James Madison) who have focused on the importance of pluralism and federalism in developing democratic societies.

James Coleman (1988) at the University of Washington found that corporation's need to improve four categories of capital in order to succeed in today's hypercompetitive global environment:

1. *Financial*
2. *Biophysical*
3. *Human, and;*
4. *Social capital.*

Executives, today, are focusing on customer and employee relationship management as the post-pandemic alters the way that they do business. Social capital stresses the critical role that executives place on relationships but most of the thought-process of this idea was pre-pandemic. In the post-pandemic, social capital may be more important than ever because leaders are continuously influencing relationships and providing valuable resources for remote worker success. Executives can change the culture of a company to shift to the new remote workplace by building trust and confidence of sustainability of not only the organization but also the employee's career. In the Post-pandemic, some workers are being labeled as remote, indefinitely. Is this a positive outcome of Covid-19? Yes. The reason being that social capital is different from human capital in that human capital focuses on individual behavior and knowledge while social capital emphasizes relationships and the assets created by these relationships. Working from home has some benefits as workers can work on a real-time basis and change things in meetings on documents for agreement and with confidence of social approval. When determining if an employee should return to work or remain remote, decisions are based upon the value added. Some firms view employees as assets, by doing this, they are treating human capital as an individual quality. Nothing wrong with human capital, which is now based on the socializing via phone and video conferences. Many employees already have returned to work because social capital is considered the quality that appears in interactions throughout the organizations and decisions are being made in-person as executives monitor safety and security. The pandemic proved to executives that when it comes to work itself, remote workers may be beneficial. Realizing that relationships and interactions are a form of capital that can help the organization become more productive and prosperous.

Executives have become more involved with social capital in the post-pandemic as they attempt to provide further opportunities and information sharing remotely that would happen naturally when in the office setting. The post-pandemic opened a whole new playing field that sheds light not only on social capital but also human capital to provide further information and opportunities for all employees when working remotely. Social capital is a resource that is found in social structures and relationships and can flourish in a remote or hybrid work environment. Social capital, when harnessed, improves information sharing.

In *Making Democracy Work*, Robert Putnam (1993), illustrates that participation and group-associated activities can increasingly internalize reciprocity to enhance trust among participants. Trust today is tantamount as employees fear losing their job due to the impact of the pandemic. They also feel that preferring to remain remote when required to return to the office may be detrimental to their career. In fact, social capital is a by-product of trust in organizations. In *Bowling alone: the collapse and revival of American community*, Putnam (2000), describes a newer approach in the social capital view that is currently known as a group perspective toward social capital. This is so important today as the post-pandemic reveals a new workplace scenario.

Back in 2000, when Putnam revealed his ideas about social capital, critics surfaced indicating that people do not engage in networks to generate trust. Instead, the critics felt that people participate in creditable groups and communities to interact with others. As a result, critics fostered a global view of social capital, advancing the social capital view through extending it to not only for individuals but also groups and societies. Propel us forward twenty-one years, and the post-pandemic is filled with groups of people attempting to conduct the same business they did pre-pandemic but now in remote groups. Still in a flux, executives want to know how social capital can be defined and used in companies. One scholar by the name of Paul Adler (2002), at the University of Southern California, illustrates how social capital could be defined, and he offers implications that can enhance organizational performance. Social Capital influences career success and executive compensation, helps workers find jobs and provides a richer pool of recruits for firms, facilitates intellectual capital, and reduces turnover rates.

Post-pandemic Application of the Social Capital View

Executives can focus on the critical role of social networks in developing relationships with other communication tools in order to enhance the performance of individuals and groups in the new hybrid work environment by managing social networks. Fostering mutual and institutionalized relationships among followers. Thus, social capital helps secure benefits, reveals new and better social networks, enhancing operational risk management and providing organizations with resilience.

The collective action of combining knowledge and

power to disseminate information and ideas quickly throughout the organization can be used as an asset when competing with rivals. Since internal structures have changed due to remote workers, the focus is on improving cohesiveness in order to achieve organizational goals remotely. Michael Woolcock, in 1998, at Brown University, illustrates how executives use social capital as a value-based approach, building trust and establishing norms of reciprocity that emerge in naturally formulated social networks.

Executives found that trust and shared values are key to success in the post-pandemic. Building trust-based relationships using social capital helps in managerial decision making, planning, and executing strategy. Knowledge emerges in interaction and socialization processes are a precursor to create knowledge, facilitates knowledge, and the social entity creates and transfers knowledge. All valuable tools that surfaced in the post-pandemic.

In Summary

Executives can improve knowledge sharing and subsequently develop participation in social networks by facilitating and fostering a culture that enables followers to socialize in a trusting and supportive environment. Thus, effective networkers who become role models and are admired and respected.

Clearly, a post-pandemic approach to social capital is an approach that encourages executives to adopt an active leadership role in the post-pandemic. This will inspire their followers to develop trust-based relationships by keeping them highly engaged with their work. Social capital is, therefore, social networks characterized by trust and shared values that help workers understand the norms that propel cooperation, build camaraderie, and extend knowledge management.

***

Chapter 7

Transformational Leadership in a Post-Pandemic World

*I*n the last chapter, we focused on Social Capital. This chapter provides more comprehensive understanding of the relationships between transformational leadership and social capital.

COVID-19 has disrupted the way business is conducted. Since March 2020, many organizations worldwide were forced to reconfigure the delivery of products or services, and operational risk shifted to include resilience. Three trends operationalized quickly. The C-Suite made a move to develop better ways to communicate electronically; they created remote teams and systematic response systems and set up a social capital playing field for leadership and follower communication.

Leadership and the Social Architect

"Good leaders are organizational architects because they know how to organize and mobilize followers so that their energies are focused on the strategic mission," (Clawson, 2021, p. 63). Transformational leadership theory highlights the importance of employee's attitudes and values in achieving organizational goals and highlights how effective organizational change is related to developing and maintaining social capital and trust in both followers and leaders.

Why is transformational leadership important to executives? Transformational leadership relies on the correlation and link between fostering people to become the best they can be. Then moves them beyond their own self-interests and links the individual interests to the collective interests of the organization. By enhancing both human capital and social capital to implement change to create valuable resources for the organization, executives realize that transformational leaders build a strong competitive advantage. This approach builds both community and solidarity to achieve the organizational mission.

We must not assume that the organizational mission is based on the organizational man (or woman). Regarded as one of the most important sociological and business commentaries of modern times, The Organization Man developed the first thorough description of the impact of mass organization on American society. During the height of the Eisenhower administration, corporations appeared to provide a blissful answer to postwar life with the marketing of new technologies—television, affordable cars, space travel, fast food—and lifestyles, such as carefully planned suburban communities centered around the nuclear family. William H. Whyte found this phenomenon alarming. Whyte was well placed to observe corporate America; it became clear to him that the American belief in the perfectibility of society was shifting from one of individual initiative to one that could be achieved at the expense of the individual. Thus, to eradicate Whyte's assumptions, the American workplace has undergone massive changes (Whyte, 2002). And, in 2007, Jon Pemberton, Sharon Mavin, and Brenda Stalker, found that:

Communities of practice are groups of like-minded people

whose interconnectedness requires a form of leadership in which the freedom to explore new ideas and set its own agenda, free from the shackles of organizational missives, has been achieved by the commitment of its members and facilitated by a coordinator acting as a leader for the purposes of organizing meetings.

Thus, as executives bring people together, either remotely, or face-to-face, they intend to improve communication as an important component of social networking. This intention is based upon sharing knowledge, building a social network of dedicated workers, and by giving them a voice in decision-making. Voice is key for buy-in and dedication to the organizational mission with less emphasis on the organizational man (woman).

A major tenet of Transformational Leadership is ***Intellectual stimulation,*** which is one way to manage a workforce better. Intellectual stimulation opens opportunity to learn and grow and this is important. By facilitating knowledge sharing and enhancing collaboration among followers and stakeholders, executives can stay on the cutting edge of industry standards and meet the demands of the post-pandemic. Elayne Coakes and Peter Smith, in 2007, posit that transformational leadership theory is appropriate for contributing to communities of practice through developing innovative workplaces in which organizational knowledge is shared by encouraging participation in social networks.

Some executives are considered social architects that bring great minds together for a good cause and meet the needs of customers. David Braga, in 2002, maintains that transformational leaders are effective networkers who provide "a flow of ideas, ask the right questions, and make the most appropriate assumptions" within organizations. Some organizations have systems in place that have been used for years and the founders or past leaders recommend. Others are pre-occupied with their own leadership models that they feel more comfortable with. The adage is that if you keep doing what you have always done then you will always get what you always got.

Transformational leaders are known as encouraging the flow of ideas and increasing social capital as people are coming together online in remote meetings, email, texting, and phone. Followers, under the pressure of building relationships with colleagues and customers online perceive themselves to be more stimulated to develop trust-based relationships that create and disseminate knowledge throughout the organization when appropriate. There is a bit of apprehension online as workers communicate because things that they say or do may be scrutinized more and heard incorrectly at times. However, people will improve their online etiquette as time prevails.

In Summary

Since Transformational Leadership, social capital, competitive advantage can open up opportunities in the post-pandemic, organizations can use these tenets to avoid possible threats, such as but not limited to, take-overs, mergers, and acquisitions. Thus, transformational leadership in a post-pandemic world will prosper as organizations recover.

***

Chapter 8

Post-Pandemic Recipe for Success: Social Capital Coupled with Resilience

While there are no quick fixes to problems in business, there are methods that are tried and true that may be able to enhance the recovery. Executives are experiencing a great deal of pressure today not only on the structure and delivery of products and services but also on the remote approach to managing and leading people.

Social Capital and Resilience can help people get

behind this pandemic that has upset all of our lives. Despite of many difficulties, people will soon resume their lives as it once was. We feel that with all we have learned and the knowledge we gained, there is still an unknown future unveiling before us.

Social capital has three important dimensions that can be incorporated in the post-pandemic recovery:
- ***structural,***
- ***cognitive, and***
- ***relational.***

These three dimensions can be addressed as corporate structure shifts to the hybrid mode. Developing a new streamlined culture, strategy, and inter-company networks for all the stakeholders involved is unveiled as organizations, universities, and institutions reposition and refocus human resources.

Building Social Capital

Janine Nahapiet and Sumantra Ghoshal, in 1998, determined the three dimensions for social capital. Post-pandemic has experienced a total shift in ability, agility, and assertiveness (the three A's). Structurally, our floors were taken out from under us as we began to work from home. Workers became dependent on electronic communication while first-line employees remained in service providing for those working remotely.

Cognitively, the pandemic caused us to re-think our social capital. In which communication shifted to online with a Zoom-like meeting. Relationally, each person is finding the best way to communicate electronically and safely. Categorizing these three tenets of structural, cognitive, and relational has set up an impetus for successful survival of the post-pandemic.

The post-pandemic has created structural dimensions that caused Adaptive Leadership for organizations throughout the world. Adaptive Leadership has a unique category of how the leaders carry themselves both strategically and socially. The Adaptive Theory emerged, in 1994, out of Ron Heifetz's book *"Leading Without Easy Answers."* Thought leaders, at that time, felt that the connections between leadership, adaptation, systems, and change were the way of the future. Unbeknown to the authors, this model of leadership became useful in the post-pandemic. Some of the important tenets of **Adaptive Leadership** are:

- Identifying challenges
- Regulating distress
- Maintain discipline and attention

- Giving the work back to the people
- Protect leadership voices from below.

Adaptive Leadership can be enhanced with social capital, which portrays an "overall pattern of connections" among employees (Choi, 2002). The speed of setting up and attending meetings during the post-pandemic is improved by having access to other employees quickly and enhanced through highly flexible structures that remote working provides. Catherine Wang and Pervaiz Ahmed (2003) indicate that highly flexible structures such as organic structures may be prone to better socialization among organizational departments and business units.

Since the pandemic, a forced decentralization of employees is enacted organically. Structural aspects of formalization and centralization that negatively relate to the structural dimension of social capital theory have been shelved as many employees are working remotely. As the C-Suite plans for the post-pandemic to stay remote or go hybrid in the future, there is still an in-conference mode for many organizations. Organizations that fail to adjust to the new technology and communication systems or that do not have the resources and leadership to adapt to their environment may not survive.

Although, the cognitive dimension was mentioned around 1998, it surfaces as an important concern since it is causing so much confusion and stress during the pandemic. Individual feelings of despair as people face uncertainty of not only the organization's in which they work, but also their own prosperity. Many people shifted their mind-set from expansive consumption to frugal purchases, less driving, more saving, and most importantly, less travel. To offset these personal feelings of dissatisfaction among employees, leaders can create an atmosphere in which followers feel more confident with remote or online communication technology, develop more trust in their organizational leaders, and, most importantly, their job security.

In general, the aggregate jobs have been maintained except for pre-determined job loss due to the natural progression of tightening the work force that was determined pre-pandemic. Post-pandemic shifts may take place as leaders determine the adjustable outcomes of the way to conduct business in the future. People are accustomed to working remotely now and some may not have to return to the office again. Barring this idea, as mentioned, there were jobs that may have been on the chopping block pre-pandemic, which may have to be revisited. Thus, the cognitive or thinking dimension of followers is defined as a shared vision, with multiple interpretations, and pertinent feelings among employees (Nahapiet & Ghoshal, 1998).

The post-pandemic caused leaders to reevaluate how they feel about their career, the industry they belong to, and the safety of work and travel. In 1985, a prominent management scholar, Edgar Schein, defined organizational culture as "the correct way to perceive, think, and feel" in order to solve organizational problems. Leaders are attempting now to find the **new best way** when there is no one-best-way to conduct business in the post-pandemic.

The post-pandemic has alluded to trust as people feel their future is compromised in some way. Trust in career progress, career attainment, career advancement, and trust in the ongoing progress of business. This is not a new issue, however, in 1993, scholars by the name of Robert Putnam, Robert Leonardi, and Raffaella Nanetti, found that "trust is an essential component of social capital." They argued that trust enhances interactions among employees. With the pandemic wielding its ugly head, people honestly lost trust in the way business is run.

With social capital at stake in the post-pandemic, trust is resurfacing as a very important concern. Organizations have an opportunity to preserve their brand and logo by making the right choices and doing the right thing. Keeping people safe, first and foremost, is the right thing to do. In 2015, Ester Villalonga-Olives and Ichiro Kawachi considered trust as an important facilitator of social capital. Thus, the post-pandemic requires cooperation, and cooperation demands collaborative behaviors, and this means people adapt to the new normal of remote work in solidarity.

Salvador Avila Cobo, in 2005, argued that collaboration is a strong determinant of "the very existence, strength, and durability of social capital." Thus, we need the cognitive dimension of social capital to help us seek a shared vision of trust, reliability, and safety. This shared vision is a mutual understanding toward determined goals, and this common perception could be reached through developing new learning opportunities through electronic leadership. Trust, collaboration, and learning how to succeed in the post-pandemic may be positively associated with the cognitive dimension of social capital theory as people change the way they think and feel about remote and hybrid work assignments.

The post-pandemic caused many people to rely on their wireless service at home, a hotspot, and cellphones. This adds another dimension to loyalty and dedication to one's career as people fund this with their home resources.

The relational dimension focuses on the importance of relationships developed in remote sessions, and argues that relations based on work obligations, reciprocity among all participants, and how to separate organizational assets from home-owned assets. Rewards and recognition need to be formalized for the home-office remote worker that is dedicating home networks to work related meetings and workflow. This has been taken for granted. However, what if a person does not have to capacity to find wireless communication at home or it is down for an hour, a day, a week, or longer? These questions have not surfaced in the business world yet and the post-pandemic will only get more challenging if these questions remain dormant.

Organizations are living breathing silos that have obligations. This is not new, in 1998, Janine Nahapiet and Sumantra Ghoshal defined obligations as "a commitment or duty to undertake some activity in the future." What defines an organization that is housed in people's home offices and kitchens? An interesting concept that needs further investigation.

Employees have a due diligence to put in the necessary effort to help the organization prosper and, during the post-pandemic, in order for a company to prosper, executives must develop a strong organizational strategy that includes both in-office and remote work---a hybrid. Daft (1995) argued that organizational strategy is evaluated as "a plan for interacting with competitive environments to achieve organizational goals." The post-pandemic organizational strategy highlights the critical role of relations with external factors and enhances social interactions with internal business units and the organizational environment in order to attain goals in the future.

With the future uncertain, organizational strategy has formulated a resilient and shared interpretation among organizational members and this positively relates to the cognitive dimension of social capital theory. Thus, the cognitive dimension is necessary for survival in the post-pandemic world because not only has the post-pandemic impacted remote work, but it also changed business-to-business transactions. This lack of business-to-business conformity is a major change in reciprocity, which stresses upon helping behavior and knowledge contribution between resources and recipients. As resilience begins to be a buzzword in the C-Suite, so many organizations are reaching out to help each other bounce back from a turbulent time of despair and safe-health considerations. We see this in our own organizations as Inter-company networks, which are a key part of relationships, and each business unit plays a critical role in enhancing knowledge transference among leaders, followers, and stakeholders.

In 2003, two scholars, Elinor Ostrom and T. K. Ahn illustrated that inter-company networks are a crucial condition for reciprocity, and they highlighted the importance of inter-company networks in creating reciprocity. Earlier, around 1988, James Coleman argued that inter-company networks facilitate access to other employees and resources, and this could improve structural social capital, which is highly affected by having access to other people quickly. With the instantaneous internet connection and the ability to create a meeting in seconds, connections are made, and knowledge is shared quickly and efficiently in the *Hallway Highway*. Thus, social capital theory in inevitably a true redeeming feature to help global resilience or organizations to bounce back. In effect "the core idea of social capital theory is that networks have value," (Robert Putnam, 2000), and value is an important resource when networking.

As executives begin to look at all stakeholders while embracing safety at home, they find themselves opening up and becoming more gregarious. This is one of the first times in history that organizations infiltrated homes with the effort to maintain workflow, stay safe, and keep followers employed. Thus, the stakeholder orientation is about enhancing the exchange of knowledge with various stakeholders. With the pandemic lurking about, executives infused what we call the **Contingency Planning Movement.** Provitera and Sayyadi (2021) argued that:

> Opening up a business enterprise too soon may be risky but keeping businesses closed too long could be costly. Figuring out the right strategy is causing a great deal of concern at the CEO and Board Room levels. What is the right thing to do? There is

not a definitive answer to this question except for one and only one. **Save Lives.** Saving lives will not only help our world survive this pandemic but will also help the brand live on for decades to come. The right time to open is, simply that, the right time to open and this is the *right thing to do*.

The Contingency planning movement was later altered to include resilience. Provitera and Sayyadi (2021) met with executives and found that resilience is the resonating word among executives as they recover from the pandemic.

Today, executives are facing uncertainty with a resolve to succeed safely, with honest and contrite hearts, and planning to sustain profitability while keeping customers and followers safe. It is not easy, and the challenge is heavy with a great deal of weight on their shoulders. How will the executives of today recover? One word: "**RESILIENCE**."

In Summary

With contingency planning and resilience, much of the knowledge exchanged with stakeholders is a result of social interactions between organizations and their business network. Elisabet Garriga Cots (2011), a prominent scholar on social capital theory, affirmed that the critical role of social capital highlights a strong association between the dimensions of social capital and stakeholder orientation.

Therefore, executives and senior managers model the three dimensions of social capital theory, structural, cognitive, and relational, as they realize that each dimension can be affected by company characteristics and decision-making.

Faced with the new post-pandemic organizational structure, whatever that may be. The adaptive culture, the enhanced strategic initiative of resilience, the inter-company network expansion, the stakeholder orientation, all of these and more may be the answer for success in the post-pandemic. Being equipped with technology, and social capital coupled with resilience, is a post-pandemic recipe for success.

***

Chapter 9

Building Competitive Advantage in the Post-Pandemic

Scholars have guided executive decision making with ideas, models, and theories since Socrates first taught groups of people in Greece. **Why should this matter now?** The post-pandemic has caused many executives to hover over strategies for recovery and resilience while others embrace academic ideas to help them make decisions about how to handle an unprecedented time in history.

The Resource Based View

The resource-based view (RBV) can be incorporated into organizations as a recipe for success in the post-pandemic. The resource-based view (RBV) is a managerial framework used to determine the strategic resources a firm can exploit to achieve sustainable competitive advantage. Barney's 1991 article "Firm Resources and Sustained Competitive Advantage" is widely cited as a pivotal work in the emergence of the resource-based view.

In 1959, Edith Penrose asserted that organizations are formed by a bundle of heterogeneously distributed resources that are rooted in a unique entity, which is what we call an organization. These internal resources reflect the degree to which a company can expand and determine the right pathway to success. Today, we face a post-pandemic that is unprecedented, and executives are pursing all viable options to ensure business success while addressing health concerns for stakeholders.

In Penrose's early work in the 60s and 70s, this idea of the organization led to a plethora of interest by scholars (such as Igor Ansoff, 1965; Kenneth Andrews, 1971; Charles Hofer and Dan Schendel, 1978). These scholars explored the importance of internal resources as strengths or weaknesses of firms, which resulted in four paradigms which executives call SWOT analysis (strengths, weaknesses, opportunities, and threats). Although still important to strategic management, a shift occurred in the implementation of strategic management and the resource-oriented approach was replaced by industrial organization economics (Hoskisson, Hitt, Wan & Yiu, 1999).

Industrial organizational economics took into consideration both operational risk and profitability. Today, while still the forefront of strategic management, a new word surfaced *"Resilience."* Organizations were assumed to be defenseless entities against threats like the post-pandemic, and opportunities that were once serendipitous faded to be more planned and organized. The executives that applied resilience models to this new planning and organizing succeeded while others ran the course of the organizational life cycle toward maturity and some, even death.

Thus, organizational risk-management was developed to offset problems before they occur and to adjust resources accordingly in the event of a possible threat. In the pre-pandemic world of business, the passive approach was the counterpoint of stable economic climates and centralized decision-making. As turbulence and hypercompetitiveness set in, this all changed, and operational risk management could not be a sustainable perspective that can be applied to change and to overcome challenges. Thus, the stacked option was to create a resilience model. Executives embraced resilience by seeking new ideas from colleagues, the scholars, and the Harvard Business School. The scholars responded. For example, "Indeed, in a crisis, our mental state often seems only to exacerbate an already extremely challenging situation, becoming a major obstacle in itself," (Hougaard, Carter, and Mohan, 2020).

The post-pandemic led to new technology, new ways of conducting business, and a new paradigm shift from office space to cyberspace. Executives had to find a new way to build teams as they changed to more remote work. People relied on the home network to conduct business for organizations; some expanded their bandwidth while others were already equipped. Executives, at first, where hesitant with remote work due to the loss of productivity. Using knowledge management and the implementation of technology has allowed for post-pandemic recovery. Executives were able to recreate the office feeling, virtually. In some cases, executives implemented camera use in the virtual office space, which has had a positive impact on productivity. This is not new technology, it existed for a long time now, but it was not utilized as much. For example, during the mid-1980s, scholars published a plethora of research that supported the idea of how an organization's internal resources, such as technology, could influence competitive advantage to a great extent (Lippman & Rumelt, 1982;

Barney, 1986; Teece, 1986; Dierickx & Cool, 1989).

Competitive advantage is still important today as organizations survive in a post-pandemic world. Executives were able to achieve a higher degree of competitive advantage before the pandemic using models developed for stable environments (Penrose, 1980; Wernerfelt, 1984; Conner, 1991). The "Pandemic added new focus on resilience: from 'just in time' to 'just in case.' (Barcaly's Insights, 2020). This just in case paradigm left executives salivating for more managerial implementation tools and resources. In the past, scholars responded to executive calls but there was no rush this time as the scholars themselves were impacted by the pandemic.

In 2002, Jay Barney presented executives with a slew of internal resources such as all tangible and intangible assets, follower and senior management capabilities, developmental and transferable competencies, new and more effective organizational processes, and cultural but firm attributes that provided a direct vision for the organization. This new set of tools, procedures, and ideas began to improve the firm's competitive advantage and companies went from having a competitive advantage to having a distinctive competitive advantage. This breakthrough in strategic management was set in a time of stable and moderately turbulent environments.

In the 1980s, this opened a whole new world of competition. Some organizations found their uniqueness. For example, The New York Times realized that ink was their distinctive competitive advantage over its competition because the ink did not run on the reader's hands. Today, the same serendipitous ideas are surfacing, and executives are pulling through an unprecedented time with new technology, a stronger concern for followers, and a newly designed awareness of how to meet customer needs. Ergo, resilience strategic management emerged.

The post-pandemic caused executives to begin to deal directly with the things that they can control while managing to lessen the burden of threats for things that they could not control. When the pandemic first surfaced, some CEOs felt that control was elusive and something that is challenging to manage. Those that embraced a distinctive competitive advantage or even core competitive advantages survived.

Reus, in 2004, espoused the development of internal resources that are rare and difficult to imitate. Organizations, in order to enhance their competitiveness through the post-pandemic recovery, would surface as having a distinctive competence in some area of the organization. Operational risk, which is primarily non-financial risk, still exposes organizations to complications that may impact revenue generation and sustenance. However, the resource-based view elucidates two capabilities of causal ambiguity and social complexity aimed at decreasing the risk of imitation of organizational capabilities by competitors. Thus, things such as keeping talented people and managing operational risk better, and more efficiently than competitors, could surface as a distinctive competitive advantage.

Executives began to deal with causal ambiguity on a daily basis during the pandemic in its multiple interpretations. Social complexity began to edge the room of the C-Suite as executive scrambled to maintain customers, keep all stakeholder safe, and sustain business using contingency planning. The main resource that was the focus, even tacitly, if not formally, was what Reus suggested, in 2004 that "the extent to which resources are embedded in multiple organizational members and the relationships among them." Thus, in one aspect, the post-pandemic core-competitive advantage relies within and among people. Who would realize that an idea, early in 2004, would surface as a distinctive core competitive advantage?

In Summary

The post-pandemic embraced the Resource-Based View (RBV) of strategic implementation while still using the Knowledge-Based View (KBV). Combining both for successful post-pandemic recover, with the use of technology to meet the needs of employees, suppliers, and customers, organization's increased its capability to utilize and create knowledge which is a crucial factor in a sustainable competitive advantage according to scholars, such as, Zheng, Yang, & Mclean (2010). This idea also came from the work of scholars in the 1990s up to, and, including 2004, as a firm's capabilities to allow it to leverage knowledge in a more efficient manner (Liebeskind, 1996; Grant & Baden-Fuller, 2004). Thus, leaders can now perform as catalysts to prepare for post-pandemic success when using technology, the resource-based view, and knowledge-based view.

The knowledge-based view focused on embedding knowledge in each member of the organization whether remote or in the office. This approach to strategic management uncovers tacit knowledge embedded among employees as a more important factor of competitive advantage compared to explicit knowledge. Executives therefore embraced various organizational factors affecting competitive advantage through enabling knowledge within organizations. Thus, building competitive advantage in the post-pandemic by adding more manageable control of internal resources and reducing operational risk while focusing on resilience has turned out to be a winning formula for success.

***

Chapter 10

Sustaining Competitive Advantage in the Knowledge Economy

*T*he pandemic caused executives, along with their followers, to either re-learn or teach how to use the necessary technology quickly and effectively. From **what you know, to who you know, to what to know?** Organizations created FlexPerts, or technologically savvy people, helped to secure technological insecurity among less seasoned employees while taking the more experienced workers to new heights.

Knowledge can be a multi-faceted concept and it can also be distinct from general information or data. During the post-pandemic, knowledge is quite elusive and is changing on a day-to-day basis with discontinued products and the ever-changing vast array of technology. A few decades ago, around

1997, Rudy Ruggles posited that knowledge is a blend of information, experiences, and codes. Today, knowledge is a resource that enables organizations to solve problems and create value through improved performance. Thus, using knowledge correctly during the post-pandemic will narrow the gap of success and failure and those who master it, will survive.

Executives are searching for new knowledge during the post-pandemic to capture, utilize, and enhance decision-making. They realize that knowledge resides in various areas such as management, the minds of employees, culture, structure, systems, processes, and relationships. The question is how to tap this knowledge in remote work environments. However, knowledge is not only stored within each individual but it is also based on social interactions shared among organizational members. Since organizational knowledge is a collective spirit that is elusive and always fluctuating based upon what people feel they know, want to know, and want to share, executives agreed with Haridimos Tsoukas, who in 1996, coined organizational knowledge as a collective mind, along with Kiku Jones and Lori Leonard, in 2009, positing that organizational knowledge is the knowledge that exists in the organization as a whole. Thus, as executives manage knowledge, they realize that organizational knowledge is owned and disseminated by the organization and can be disseminated by formal or informal leaders. They also realize that some knowledge may be stored away cognitively, not shared, and lost due to attritional levels quite high in the post-pandemic. Therefore, some executives have developed expert systems to tap the knowledge of highly experienced individuals. Others set up mentor systems to keep the knowledge in the organization as people retire, and, most importantly, some are gathering and storing knowledge as it is created or found.

Tacit and Explicit Knowledge

Knowledge is impromptu and hard to analyze, interpret, and even solicit in organizations. Then we have tacit knowledge, which is more elusive than knowledge in general. The difference being that tacit knowledge is not shared by many individuals, because it is either dormant in their subconscious or people are too shy to express what they know. Some people, honestly and contritely, do not like to express themselves in organizations. The lack of fluent knowledge in organizations causes a bottleneck. To offset possible bottlenecks of knowledge fluency, executives attempt to manage knowledge to enhance productivity along with individual performance, limit turf issues in the organization, build and keep customer satisfaction, and nurture stakeholder value.

Leaders must learn to tap the knowledge of followers

and reward bursts of contribution to the organization. Celebrating minor successes in knowledge bursts can place an organization with a competitive advantage in the forefront of the post-pandemic. Schoemaker (2021) states that "all of you [followers] are the eyes and ears of the organization, and not only you internally, but all of you have contacts, children, families, that read the news and watch television, there is a disconnect is un-closed loops of knowledge transfer both up and down the organization." This disconnect needs to be shattered for organizations to succeed in the post-pandemic world. An example of leadership and knowledge, noted by Paul Schoemaker, on March 23, 2021, is how executives plan on how to rebound. During the COVID-19 crisis, very few companies had a sound plan. Few companies had rebounding programs with the role of boards and C-Suites. Schoemaker states that **whatever does not kill you makes you stronger afterwards**. Most organizations do not have this capability. Learning from each challenge is key."

The post-pandemic revealed that scenario planning is crucial to advancing protocol and estimating what are necessary actions in the future. Day and Schoemaker, in 2019, found that "Vigilant firms have greater foresight than their rivals, while vulnerable firms often miss early signals of external threats and organizational challenges."

Developing views about the future, focusing on, as best

as you can on what you can and cannot control. Preparing as best as possible to absorb the things that you cannot control in a positive way is key to survival in the post-pandemic world. Both short term and long-term planning can save people's jobs, create new ventures, and sustain a business over the long run. Short-term goals have been stymied in the uncertainty of the post-pandemic and executives must extrapolate probability to forecast the future.

Although, the extent of ambiguity, not knowing enough, wreaks havoc in the C-Suite and beyond, some organizations are finding ample ways to recover. Academics may want to tell you about things they know, empirical studies, theories, and they do not want to talk about what they do not know. Thus, scholars are attempting to forecast new business horizons along with executives.

Strengths, Weaknesses, Opportunities, and Threats, (SWOT), emphasize the status quo, the past, and the future. Digging out skeletal closets and redesigning organizational charts coupled with advancing opportunities for the future while avoiding both known and unknown threats is the new SWOT analysis. SWOT scenario planning has limitations and as mentioned earlier, resilience is key to the SWOT analysis that will help organizations prevail as they recover. Vigilance is only as good as what you are vigilant about at a particular time. Vigilant about the wrong things could be disastrous yet vigilance about the right things can be time-consuming. The best advice here is to focus on who to collaborate with (best practices), what to extrapolate on (product or service enhancement), and how can organizations help each other without hurting the bottom line (i.e., MBWAIG – Management By Wandering Around Industry Giants). Organizations can all grow together, or they may face the wrath of the organizational life cycle and eventually die. Come together in industrial solidarity or fail as an individual organization.

Since tacit knowledge is knowledge that exists in the minds of organizational members which is gained by their individual experiences and is difficult to formalize and transfer unless directed to do so, executives need to pinpoint and encourage this type of knowledge to be drawn out of followers. Kirk Landon, founder of Assurant Solutions, in South Florida, created a suggestion box. This was not your normal suggestion box. It was a think-tank in which he wanted to see every suggestion that a leader, or immediate supervisor, turned down. Tapping tacit knowledge this way attempts to steep lower in organizational echelon to the front-line employees. The ones that are on the frontline, a term used very often in post-pandemic. Frontline employees need to be held on a pedestal as they not only kept themselves safe, but also kept the quarantined employees fortified with food, clothing, and the day-to-day needs to operate safely in a remote setting.

The suggestion box idea is well-thought out by Landon, but how else can tacit knowledge be ascertained. Mike Provitera told a reporter "If you're asked in a meeting or at a social function (for example, at Morgan Stanley, Inc., the CEO had a program called "Breakfast with the CEO") about new ideas, then it is okay to bring your idea up," Richmond (2014). In many instances, people hold back ideas because they feel that they may not be implemented or even accepted in any way. While organizations are thriving to become more decentralized, unfortunately, the centralized workplace still exists today when it comes to innovation and creativity.

In the post-pandemic, the more controllable, explicit knowledge is utilized. Explicit knowledge is the type of knowledge that is highly formalized and codified and can be easily recorded and communicated through formal and systematic language and manifested in rules and procedures providing the necessary tools and processes for executives to manage. It can also be captured in expert systems and tapped into by many people throughout the organization via intranets and organizational databases. Thus, explicit knowledge is more formal and has the potential to be more easily shared and, in some instances, it can be useful compared to tacit knowledge. Jim Clawson, in his latest book, "Level Three Leadership: How to Become an Effective Executive," provides a lifelong journey of antidotes, models, stories, challenges for the executive mindset. More work like this must be done.

The Future of Private and Public Knowledge

Public knowledge is on the forefront of the news today as executives decide upon the post-pandemic scheduling of workers, how to deliver products, provide services, and bask in the plethora of important decisions for recovery. Many organizations are pondering what future strategic initiatives regarding remote work will look like. For example, some executives may incorporate a hybrid model, for example, two days on, with three days off during the week. Others are contemplating no-zoom Fridays. Jamie Dimon, in an article published by Quartz, in April 2021, expresses hesitations about working from home. He is not the only one, either. Goldman Sachs' David Solomon called remote work an "aberration" and said he does not want another class of young people arriving at Goldman in the summer, of 2021, remotely. Barclays CEO Jes Staley anticipates his staff of 80,000 to return to the office sometime in 2021. Thus, there may be a mixture of office-bound, hybrid, and fully remote employees in the post-pandemic. Either way, the world of work has changed forever due to COVID-19.

Since executives are constantly dealing with the public messaging systems, Wall-Street Analysts, and especially if the organization is publicly traded on the New York Stock Exchange, they must be vigilant to what is printed and captured on social media. The private and public knowledge is something they pay a great deal of attention to in the C-Suite.

In 1998, a scholar, Sharon Matusik, argued that knowledge in organizations can be categorized as either private or public knowledge and can be advantageous to executive decision-making. Firm specific knowledge must be guarded and not shared with the competition. Any leak of such information may expose the organization and increase operational risk. Contrary to private knowledge, public knowledge differs in that it is not unique for any organization and industry analysts and reporters have free reign to opine, forecast, and extrapolate corporate decisions. Public knowledge, when positive, may be an asset and provide potential benefits when posted in social media and other means of communication. When negative, could destroy a company.

The ownership of knowledge is a factor, which is a significant contributor to the knowledge of organizations, and, in many cases, it is intellectual property. Intellectual property is considered equity and is very valuable to organizations. Executives know which knowledge should remain private and which to go public with. A mistake in this area may be fatal to the organization. The post-pandemic has opened a slew of communication focusing on contingency planning, resilience, recovery, and most importantly, safety. A day does not pass without hearing something about the post-pandemic. Positive information or not, this is a way of life now as advertisers, and the media, will continue to address current events as they unfold.

A Look at Individual and Collective Knowledge in the Post-Pandemic

Knowledge can be classified into individual and collective. For example, executives recruit followers based on their individual knowledge, which refers to the individual's skills, prior-knowledge, and proficiencies, which is sometimes referred to as leadership and managerial competencies. Collective knowledge has been defined as "organizing principles, routines, and practices, top management schematics, and relative organizational consensus based upon past experiences, goal orientation, organizational mission and vision statements, industry competitors, and relationships that are widely diffused throughout the organization and held in common by a large number of organizational members (Matusik, 1998). Collective knowledge is part of the executive's protocol and comes fairly natural to the leaders at the higher echelons of the organization. At lower levels of the organization, knowledge is approached with trepidation, with a check and verify component, to avoid divulging the wrong information or avoiding a careless approach to expose things that need to remain internal.

In 1988, many executives followed Thomas Davenport and Laurence Prusak's concern that if an executive cannot inspire its followers to share their individual knowledge with others, then this individual knowledge is not valuable to the organization. This caused a wide influx of new technology, focus groups, and employee engagement. The reason being is that Individual knowledge can become a valuable resource by developing an organizational climate of openness for members to exchange their ideas and insights. This is tantamount to the Hawthorne Experiments conducted by Elton Mayo and his colleagues at Harvard Business School in the Hawthorne Plant in Chicago. People responded positively to discussions over tea and coffee, which led the Human Relations Movement.

Thus, executives that create a climate of trust and openness for individuals to share individual knowledge have been able to tap into innovative and novel ideas. In the post-pandemic, new technologies draw on social-software systems that share individual knowledge. This positively contributed the post-pandemic recovery, as organizations began to create collective knowledge that enhanced remote work and virtual training platforms. Executives that build an atmosphere of trust and openness coupled with the use of technology to convert individual knowledge into valuable resources for their organization will help organizations prosper in the post-pandemic world.

A Look at Individual, Social, and Structured Knowledge in the Post-Pandemic

Knowledge can also be classified using individual, social, and structured dimensions. Executives can categorize followers based on their human knowledge, which focuses on individual knowledge and manifests itself in individual's competencies and skills. A knowledge organizational chart can be created to celebrate the vast knowledge in an organization. This form of knowledge comprises the skills gained by individual experience and learned as rules and instructions formulated by executives for followers to use as a guide. Social knowledge, on the other hand, is categorized as individual knowledge that is shared so that it can become collective knowledge.

Executives can use structured knowledge, which emerges in formal language from annual reports, memos, and other means of communication to be represented as statements that can be easily retrieved. In comparison with human, technical, and conceptual skills, executives can classify knowledge in this way so that it emerges at all three levels----individual (i.e., human), group (i.e., social), and organizational (i.e., structured). Human skills are used at all levels of the organization with technical skills used more at lower echelons of the organization, and conceptual skills at the executive level of the organization.

The difference in the post-pandemic is that there is now a level playing field. Giving people center stage when on zoom-type related meetings. This factor has highlighted the person's attention to knowledge, as more people feel comfortable with electronic communication. However, this could also be a drawback. When people express themselves in a zoom-type meeting, they may come off as standoffish or counter-productive. There is a fine line of expressing knowledge in zoom type meetings. A new savvy approach to communication exists. One in which employees are becoming aware of what they say and know what they say matters. Being cautious to the online meeting limelight is important, however. There is a savvy approach to online meetings. Listening more than speaking, being courteous to others as people may want to speak at the same time, and most importantly, realizing that online meetings are not the same as face-to-face. The fact that a screen awaits your commentary does not take away from what you say, what you do, or what you act like. Be very careful to not come off the wrong way and always be courteous and concerned for the people you speak to. You career depends on it.

The Post-Pandemic and Scientific, Philosophical, and Commercial Knowledge

The post-pandemic has created a broad base of knowledge, which is indicative of scientific, philosophical, and commercial knowledge that executives are aware of in today's hypercompetitive business environment. From vaccines to the philosophy of survival, to widespread mass communication about chemistry, knowledge is spread quickly, and the rumor mill may distort information being encoded. Scientific knowledge is objective and manifests itself as provable and verifiable knowledge or truth, while philosophical knowledge clarifies that "truth is embedded in language and therefore inaccessible" (Demarest, 1997). The key for executives is manage both scientific and philosophical knowledge so that commercial knowledge is focused upon, enhancing effective performance.

During the post-pandemic, commercial knowledge has been in effect, as many workers conduct their work functions remotely. Commercial knowledge empowers the capabilities of an organization, and actively improves its competitive advantage in the marketplace by taking an objective approach. Objectivity, as opposed to a subjective approach to knowledge can positively contribute to a firm's performance. Thus, executives are finding novel ways to use commercial knowledge; they are enhancing it and distributing it. Capturing knowledge in real-time so that there is a seamless transition from remote work to returning to the office or some hybrid approach.

Knowledge Management in the Post-Pandemic

Before COVID-19, the pre-pandemic, the drive was to strongly enhance customer relationship management, after the global shutdown of March 2020; knowledge management became an enabler for identifying and satisfying customer's needs and manifested itself as a significant driver that motivates the development of relationships with customers. Organizations no longer had the opportunity for face-to-face convenience after government mandates to work remotely except for the front-line workers. These workers need to be paid tribute for the cause that they propelled forward to keep products and services fluid in the mist a worldwide pandemic.

The convenience of meeting face-to-face was shelved for online orders, deliveries, and meeting virtually in zoom-type meetings. Scholars proved to executives that they can use knowledge management to improve customer satisfaction through acquiring additional knowledge from customers, developing better relationships with existing customers, and providing a higher quality of products and services for them using electronic and carrier delivery. This was not a new concept, but it was abbreviated at the time. The pandemic changed everything, forever.

Knowledge management is used in the post-pandemic to help executives with employee development, hiring, firing, training, and building camaraderie. Webinar type training is becoming the forefront to success in organizations worldwide and those who train well survive. Many successful training sessions have exemplified a motto that is true but not regularly considered. A common concept not commonly used. "***If you train people, they may leave but if you do not train them, they may stay, forever untrained***." Some organizations are ill equipped to meet and exceed the competitive pressure of sustainable business ventures in the post-pandemic. They find that they are continuously jockeying for market share that is becoming narrow for many organizations.

Because training is not at the forefront of the post-pandemic recover, it is shelved for more strategic issues to remain afloat in a wide sea of icebergs. Thus, the return on investment to shareholders for training is not transparent and some executives forfeit training opportunities in lieu of profit generating efforts. Smart executives, however, during the post-pandemic, keep employees adept on the new technology and provide webinar training. Losing a year of training and development can move a front-runner into second place and, in some cases, leave organizations behind in which their competitive presence is dismal.

Learning and developing people is a process that leads to acquiring new insights and knowledge, and potentially to correct sub-optimal or ineffective actions and behaviors that cause companies to spiral out of control. The post-pandemic found many organizations facing chapter 11. Just one year into the pandemic, left some organizations on Main Street, in bankruptcy (Chapter 11 of the United States Bankruptcy Code permits reorganization under the bankruptcy laws of the United States). This means that all debts may be managed while the organization prepares for survival or decides to dismantle operations and close. Similar codes exist globally to help global organizations survive. Here is a list of all the major companies that have filed for bankruptcy so far since the coronavirus pandemic hit the United States (nbcnews.com, by Emily Pandise, May 15, 202, Updated March 9, 2021).

- Dean and Deluca
- Apex Parks
- Foodfirst, Bravo and Brio Restaurant Parent
- True Religion Apparel
- CMX Cinemas
- Rubie's Costume Company
- J. Crew
- Gold's Gym

- Neiman Marcus
- Stage Stores
- JCPenny
- Pier 1 Imports
- Hertz
- Tuesday Morning
- Le Pain Quotidien
- 24 Hour Fitness
- GNC

The post-pandemic shakeout spared none. Every organization felt the impact of the pandemic in some way. If you are an executive struggling to hold down the fort, there is help and one fact is that there is a relationship between knowledge management and organizational learning. Mastering these two tenets can make ordinary organizations extraordinary.

In 2005, Hari Bapuji Bayyavarapu suggested a learning-based approach to knowledge management to understand how organizational learning is related to various processes of knowledge management. Surviving organizations today managed to effectively implement knowledge management by sharing the best practices and experiences among employees and thus enhanced overall organizational performance. However, as the post-pandemic surrounds the C-Suite with new information daily, a more comprehensive model needs to be introduced to put together the various aspects of potential contributions to organizational performance for post-pandemic recovery.

Industry research conducted by Adela Lau and Eric Tsui (2009) showed that effective organizational learning requires various processes such as knowledge acquisition, collaboration, dissemination, sharing, generation, and storage to acquire knowledge within an organization. Thus, using technology such as but not limited to Microsoft Teams, Zoom, Skype, has helped executives improve not only the use of knowledge management but also improved organizational processes through various practices. The training and development, which is not getting much attention today, can also enhance organizational learning and increase both follower engagement and personal development, which can help organizations survive.

Customer Relationship Management: A Knowledge Management Perspective

Executives are spending a great deal of time today on operational risk management. Resilience has added more airtime to the operational-risk scenario. Operational risk, according to Karl Wiig (1994), is an operational approach to represent knowledge management but in this case, it seeks to apply organizational knowledge in order to satisfy and exceed customer's expectations (Keskin 2005). Resilience, or Operational Resilience, has surfaced not only for the financial sector but also for Main Street.

> Even prior to the Covid-19 pandemic, the Committee considered that significant operational disruptions would inevitably test improvements to the financial system's resilience made since the Great Financial Crisis (GFC) of 2007-2009. As the Covid-19 pandemic progressed, the Committee observed banks rapidly adapting their operational posture in response to new hazards or changes in existing hazards that occurred in different parts of their organization. Recognizing that a range of potential hazards cannot be prevented, the Committee believes that a pragmatic, flexible approach to operational resilience can enhance the ability of banks to withstand, adapt to and recover from potential hazards and thereby mitigate potentially severe adverse impacts. (www.bis.org).

The knowledge economy has opened up a new form of leadership, electronic leadership. Leaders are surrounding themselves by remote workers that are taking the lead on projects, making final decisions, voicing business and environmental concerns, and stepping up to take on more leadership roles. Facilitating more is the new way of leading in the post pandemic world.

The post-pandemic has also given rise to a new customer experience. One in which there is very little to no contact with people, yet the same products and services are desired. Thriving organizations are finding new ways to meet customer needs virtually. Thus, similar to customer relationship management, knowledge management is an enabler for identifying and satisfying customer's needs and manifests itself as a significant driver that motivates the development of relationships with customers. Executives are using knowledge management to improve customer satisfaction through acquiring additional knowledge from customers, developing better relationships with them, and providing a higher quality of service and/or products for them (North, Reinhardt, and Schmidt, 2004; Sukumaran et al. 2009).

Employee development and training has been challenged in the post-pandemic. The in-house trainings came to a halt in March of 2020 but a rise in training and development is slowly picking up. Look at the names of these training sessions and you feel like a whole new opportunity to learn and grow in the post-pandemic exists. Timely training---in person and online---for essential business skills that are in-demand and increasingly important touts a leading training company.

- Covid Workplace Safety
- Dealing with Difficult Customers During COVID-19
- HR's Role in COVID-19, How Human Resources is Establishing the New Normal
- How Teachers Can Instruct and Engage Students with Online Learning
- Managing Virtual Employees
- How to Deliver Engaging and Interactive Online Training
- Maximizing Productivity with Microsoft Teams
- Best HR Practices for Communicating with Remote Employees
- Best Practices for Transitioning Work from Your Office to the Kitchen Counter
- Families First Coronavirus Response ACT (FFCRA), Exploring the Emergency Leave Acts: A Virtual "Town-Hall" Meeting
- HR, Title VII Laws and Virtual Meetings
- How Emotions Drive Decision-Making During a Crisis
- Stress Management During a Crisis
- Support for the Home Office: Strategies for Communicating and Assisting Employees during the COVID-19 Quarantine

- Tips for a Successful Home Office with Kids in the House.

Such an exhausting list of how-to-handle the post-pandemic world in which we live and work. Providing the emphasis on knowledge once again as the world comes out of a huge crisis. The key function of knowledge management is to help executives with employee development. In our contextual world of uncertainty, training is becoming the forefront to success in organizations worldwide. The more training the better the return on investment to shareholders which is imperative to sustain the business. Learning is a process that leads to acquiring new insights and knowledge, and potentially to correct sub-optimal or ineffective actions and behaviors that cause organizations to spiral out of control (Dorfler, 2010).

Today, executives are realizing that learning is "a dynamic process of strategic renewal occurring across three levels of the organization (i.e. the individual, the online-groups, and the organization where ever that may reside), leading to change in cognitional behaviors, as well as closing the performance gap between success and failure" (Crossan, Lane & White 1999).

Executives have found that organizational learning

results in newer insight and knowledge. Thus, changing of the existing behaviors of followers and generating new knowledge. Thus, learning is a key factor in improving a firm's competitive advantage (Linderman et al. 2004). Understand how organizational learning is related to various processes of knowledge management (Bayyavarapu, 2005), and how learning can be sustained and perhaps increased in a virtual workplace will be tantamount in the post-pandemic. As new technological products surface, the effective implementation of knowledge management requires learning and sharing of best practices and experiences among employees and thus enhances overall organizational performance (Vera & Crossan 2003; Yang, 2004; Bayyavarapu 2005).

Organizational learning is "a set of actions (i.e., knowledge acquisition, information distribution, information interpretation, and organizational memory) within the organization that intentionally and, in some cases, unintentionally influence positive organizational change" (Templeton, Bruce, & Snyder 2002), as well as "a dynamic process of creation, acquisition and integration of knowledge aimed at the development of resources and capabilities that contribute to better organizational performance" (López, Peón & Ordás 2005).

In the post-pandemic, a more comprehensive model of learning and knowledge management needs to be introduced to put together the various aspects of potential contributions to organizational performance. For example, Adela Lau and Eric Tsui (2009) assert that effective organizational learning requires various processes such as knowledge acquisition, collaboration, dissemination, sharing, generation, and storage to acquire and retrieve knowledge within an organization. In some circumstances, this information must be retrieved quickly and effectively to ensure product and service success. Thus, from a technological perspective, knowledge shows that management may improve organizational processes through various Knowledge Management practices and can also enhance organizational learning that increases both follower engagement and personal development.

Embracing Knowledge Management to Satisfy and Retain Remote Workers

Knowledge management, also, to some human resource managers, known as talent management, allows for a rich basis to understanding the mechanisms by which talent management is influenced.

Talent management is an important concern with so many employees working remotely. Executives are prioritizing strategic initiatives based on each employee's experience. This enables organizations to solve problems and create value through improved performance and it is this point that will narrow the gaps of success and failure leading to more successful decision-making as the remote teams begin to dissimulate and migrate back to some sort of office setting. Executives are tailoring talent to address current goals. Future goals are set with shorter milestones of progress. For example, in the short term, executives are developing a talent acquisition strategy, which focuses on planning the work and technically supporting newly hired employees to achieve the business goals that are indicative of an ongoing remote workforce or some semblance of that. Thus, a talent acquisition strategy helps companies to achieve their business goals that reflect excellence while working remotely with an eye to easing back into the office. Talent needs to be kept current while planning for the future by stemming from a talent acquisition strategy across pivotal areas of the organization.

In the post-pandemic, hiring managers are using education as a way of familiarizing with the new way of the employee recruitment practice. Actively seeking new candidates through zoom-type interviews in our rapidly transforming workplace. New uses of technology upended how we work, where we work, why we work, and who is going to do the work. Creating implications for what leaders do now as they prepare their workforce for the very near future.

Looking at the educated pool of talent helps save training and development financing as people are hitting the ground running from their first day on the job. Education is more active, more broad, more flexible, more experimental, more synthetic, and more strategic compared to training. With new hires comes new insights and new knowledge, potentially correcting sub-optimal or ineffective actions and behaviors that cause companies to spiral out of control.

Executive demonstration of modeling innovative behavior will motivate employees to approach organizational problems in a more novel way. Inspiring employees to rethink problems and challenge their current personal attitudes and values toward work. Change beliefs, if necessary, so that new hires are willing to perform beyond their previous level.

In the post-pandemic, there is a virtual shift, which impacts global workplace presence. This flexibility in the workplace may enable executives to improve departmental and managerial interactions and develop relationships among managers, including more business units, and departments. Flexibility is the new norm today as people work from their home office, kitchen table, or closet. Many executives are shifting the power of decision-making to the lower levels and inspire newly hired employees to create new ideas and then follow through and implement them, which can in turn propel interdepartmental communications and improve knowledge exchange.

The key is to use the effects of knowledge

management with talent management. Trends are re-imagining executive education, and program delivery has shifted in the post-pandemic world. Sawhney (2021) argues that "while the past year has been a time of great challenge...it has also been a time of great innovation." He states 3 horizons of change that will impact both executives and talent management in the near future:

1) Reacting to the pandemic – transforming to exclusively online formats

2) Redesigning the future – gradually returning to in-person and hybrid work to deliver the best learning experiences.

3) Reimagining what executive education can be – reinvent and design disruptive business models and formats for executive education.

The Competitive Advantage of Knowledge Management

With "knowledge" as a strategic factor for a competitive advantage, executives are finding novel ways maintain it, store it, retrieve it, and protect it, especially in the post-pandemic. With the extent that conversations are aired online, there is the potential of hackers attempting to get into a firm's database to acquire knowledge. The post-pandemic has increased the knowledge creation and utilization pertinent to an organization's success regarding remote work platforms. Many new ideas for innovation and motivation of employees to solve their current problems and address future work-related formats in a more innovative manner. Post-pandemic, the acquisition of new knowledge is an ongoing process and can be essential to identify the needs of customers and address and recognize changes in the business environment. Thus, sustaining competitive advantage in the knowledge economy is a worthwhile investment and will pay dividends forever.

CONCLUSION

As the post-pandemic continues to unfold, executives continue to integrate knowledge internally to enhance the effectiveness and efficiencies in various systems and processes, as well as to be more responsive to market changes, knowledge integration and the accumulated knowledge is shared and synthesized with an aim to providing higher quality products and services.

Executives in the C-Suite are treading water in a world that has been stymied, turned upside down, and flipped. Jamie Dimon, JPMorgan CEO shares some concern (Cheng, 2021).

> *JPMorgan was able to quickly set up employees from call centers to trading desks to do their work from home, Dimon said, "We learned that we could function virtually with Zoom and Cisco and maintain productivity, at least in the short run."*

Shared knowledge on platforms such as Zoom, and Teams can contribute to the development of a learning organization in which people continuously grow and develop both personally and professionally. However, according to Dimon, it is only temporary to work remotely.

During the post-pandemic, the integrated knowledge needs to be reconfigured to meet environmental changes and the new challenges that arise while, at the same time, knowledge should not be leaked to the competition in any shape or form unless agreed upon by senior executives. Knowledge management, when used as a competitive advantage, can therefore improve financial and non-financial performance but, as Dimon notes, remote work has some "serious weaknesses," (Cheng, 2021):

- Performing jobs remotely is more successful when people know one another and already have a large body of existing work to do. It does not work as well when people do not know one another.

- Most professionals learn their job through an apprenticeship model, which is almost impossible to replicate in the Zoom world. Over time, this drawback could dramatically undermine the character and culture you want to promote in your company.

- A heavy reliance on Zoom meetings actually slows down decision making because there is little immediate follow-up.

- Remote work virtually eliminates spontaneous learning and creativity because you do not run into people at the coffee machine; talk with clients in unplanned scenarios or travel to meet with customers and employees for feedback on your products and services.

Mastery in the workplace in the post-pandemic, therefore, is using what worked pre-pandemic, what shifted during the pandemic, and building upon resilience to carry us through post-pandemic. Transformational leadership coupled with knowledge management paves the way of the future. Organizations must build upon existing knowledge and create new innovative and creative ways to navigate the knowledge economy.

Knowledge management coupled with transformational leadership will continue to be tweaked, extrapolated, and augmented as we navigate this unprecedented time of the post-pandemic.

***

References

Introduction

Cheng, M. (2021). "JPMorgan CEO Jamie Dimon shares his thoughts on remote work," Quartz, found on website on April 26, 2021: https://qz.com/1993431/jpmorgan-ceo-jamie-dimon-shares-his-thoughts-on-remote-work/?utm_source=email&utm_medium=quartz-at-work&utm_content=5d162eb5-9c97-11eb-83ef-56d4922740c6

Taylor, T. 2021. *New Research Shows Top Soft Skills Are Requested Four Times More Thank Top Hard Skills*. America Succeeds.

Chapter 1

Bass, BM & Stogdill RM 1990, *Bass & Stogdill's handbook of leadership: theory, research, and managerial applications*, Free Press, New York.

Bennis, W 2009, *On Becoming a Leader*, Basic Books, New York.

Bennis, W & Nanus, B 1985, *Leaders: The strategies for taking charge*, Harper, New York.

Blair, JD & Hunt, JG 1985, A research agenda for leadership on the future battlefield. In Hunt JG & Blair JD (eds.), *Leadership on the future battlefield. Pergamon*, Brassey's, Washington, DC.

Kotterman, J. (2006). "Leadership and Management: What is the Difference," Journal for Quality and Participation, 29, (2): 13-17.

Mintzberg, H 2009, *Managing*, Berrett-Koehler Publishers, Oakland, California.

Provitera, M. J 2021, *No Jerk Policy: Why People Don't Like a Jerk*, Motivational Leadership Training Publishers, Ft. Lauderdale, Florida, USA.

Rindova, VP & Starbuck, WH 1997, Distrust in dependence: The ancient challenge of superior-subordinate relations. In Advancements in Organization Behaviour: Essays in Honour of Derek Pugh C, eds C TAR (ed.), Hants7 Dartmouth Publishing, Aldershot.

Rost, JC 1991, *Leadership for the twenty-first century*, Praeger, New York.

Yammarino, F.J., Dionne, S.D., Uk, C.J., & Dansereau, F. 2005. Leadership and levels of analysis: A state-of-the-science review. *The Leadership Quarterly,* vol. 16, no. 6, pp. 879-919.

Zaleznik, A 1977, Managers and Leaders: Are They Different? *Harvard Business Review*, May-June, pp. 74-81

Chapter 2

Elliot, J & Simon, W 2011, The Steve Jobs Way : iLeadership for a New Generation, Vanguard Press, New York.

Lee, M. (2014). "Transformational Leadership: Is it Time for a Recall?" International Journal of Management and Applied Research, 1, 17-29.

Mills, DQ 2005, Leadership: How to Lead, How to Live, MindEdge Press, Waltham, MA.

Scipioni, J. (2020). "Barack Obama on the mistakes he sees leaders make," found on May 4, 2021, on website https://www.cnbc.com/2020/12/03/barack-obama-on-the-mistakes-he-sees-leaders-make.html

Teerlink, R & Ozley, L 2000 More Than a Motorcycle: The Leadership Journey at Harley-Davidson, Harvard Business School Press, Boston, MA.

Venkatraman, N. (1989). Strategic orientation of business enterprises: the construct, dimensionality, and measurement. Management Science, 35(8), 942-962.

Vozz, S. (2019). "C-Suite Thought Leadership: Making CEOs the Public Face and Voice of Your Content Marketing," found on May 4, 2021 on website https://www.skyword.com/contentstandard/c-suite-thought-leadership-making-ceos-the-public-face-and-voice-of-your-content-marketing/

Chapter 3

Acosta, A. (2019). Adaptive Leadership for Our Time, found on May 10, 2021, on website: **https://medium.com/@aa3749/adaptive-leadership-for-our-times-85c59fcf7912**

Avolio, B. J., Kahai, S., & Dodge, G. E. (2000). E-leadership: Implications for theory, research, and practice. The Leadership Quarterly, 11(4).

Bryman, A. (1992). *Charisma and leadership in organizations*, London: Sage.

Clawson, J. (2021). Fundamentals of Level Three Leadership: How to Become an Effective Executive, BusinessExpertPress, New York (Edited by Dr. Michael Provitera).

Eicher-Catt, D 2005, The myth of servant-leadership. Women and Language, vol. 28, no. 1, pp. 17-25.

Fisher, B.M., & Edwards, J.E. (1988). Consideration and initiating structure and their relationship with leader effectiveness: A meta-analysis. *Proceedings of the Academy of Management.* Anaheim, CA.

Ford, J & Harding, N 2011, The impossibility of the 'true self' of authentic leadership, Leadership, vol. 7, no. 4, pp. 463–479

García-Morales, VJ, Jiménez-Barrionuevo, MM & Gutiérrez-Gutiérrez, L 2012 Transformational leadership influence on organizational performance through organizational learning and innovation, Journal of Business Research, vol. 65, no. 7, pp. 1040-1050.

Gardiner, RA 2011, A Critique of the Discourse of Authentic Leadership, International Journal of Business and Social Science, vol. 2, no. 15, pp. 99-104.

George, B 2003, Authentic leadership: rediscovering the secrets to creating lasting value. Jossey-Bass: San Francisco, CA.

Graeff, C.L. (1997). Evolution of situational leadership theory: A critical review. *The Leadership Quarterly*, 8(2), 153-170.

Greenleaf, RK 1988, The Power of Servant-Leadership, Berrett-Koehler Publishers: San Francisco, CA.

Greenleaf, RK 1977, Servant Leadership: A Journey into the Nature of Legistimate Power and Greatness, Paulist Press: Nahwah, NJ.

Groysberg B., Abrahams, R., and Connolly Baden, K. C. The Pandemic Conversations That Leaders Need to Have Now, (April 21) Harvard Business School.

Kernis, M & Goldman, B 2006, A multicomponent conceptualization of authenticity: theory and research. In M. P. Zanna (eds.), Advances in experimental social psychology, Academic Press: San Diego.

Labrou, M. (2020). Why effective servant-leadership entails the upside-down pyramid. Found on May 12, 2020 on website: **https://www.linkedin.com/pulse/why-effective-servant-leadership-entails-upside-down-pyramid-labrou/?articleId=6677836786800070656**

Lawrence, M & Spears, LC 2004, Practicing Servant Leadership: Succeeding through Trust, Bravery, and Forgiveness, Jossey-Bass: San Francisco.

Lee, C & Zemke, R 1993, The search for spirit in the workplace, Training, vol. 30, pp. 21-28.

Lee, C & Zemke, R 1995, Reflections on leadership : how Robert K. Greenleaf's theory of Servant-leadership influenced today's top management thinkers, ., edited by Larry C. Spears, New York : John Wiley & Sons, Inc.

Likert, R. (1961). *New patterns of management*. New York: McGraw-Hill.

Lynch, M. (2016). 6 Reasons Why You Should Become a Transformational Leader, The Edvocate. Found on website **https://www.theedadvocate.org/6-reasons-why-you-should-become-a-transformational-leader/#:~:text=Transformational%20leadership%20allows%20workers%20to,organizational%20values%20to%20follower%20values** on March 3, 2021.

Marturano, A., & Gosling, J. (2008). *Leadership*, London: Routledge.

McClure, B. (2021). A Guide to CEO Compensation, Investopedia. Found on website **https://www.investopedia.com/managing-wealth/guide-ceo-compensation/** on March 4, 2021.

Murphy, A.J. (1941). A study of the leadership process. In J.L. Pierce & J.W. Newstrom (Eds.), *Leaders & the leadership process: Readings, self-assessments, & applications*, Boston, MA: McGraw-Hill/Irwin.

Murphy, B. (2019). Bill Gates Says This 1 Employee Perk Is Most Important. A New Harvard Study Backs Him Up: It turns out employees want this, and it just might make them more productive, Inc. Magazine.

Northouse, P. (2010). *Leadership: theory and practice*. Thousand Oaks, CA: Sage Publications.

Patiar, A & Mia, L 2009 Transformational leadership style, market competition and departmental performance: Evidence from luxury hotels in Australia, International Journal of Hospitality Management, vol. 28, no. 2, pp. 254-262.

Pendersen, C. L., and Ritter, T. (2020, April 10). *Preparing Your Business for a Post-Pandemic World*, Harvard Business Review.

Pierce, J.L., & Newstrom, J.W. (2008). *Leaders & the leadership process: Readings, self-assessments & applications*. Boston, MA: McGraw-Hill, Irwin.Yoon, KS 2005 Testing the Firestone and McElroy Knowledge Management Model: An Empirical Study, State University of New York.

Sims, H.P., Faraj, S., & Yun, S. (2009). When should a leader be directive or empowering? How to develop your own situational theory of leadership. *Business Horizons*,

52(2), 149-158.

Smith, N. R., and Miner, J. B. (1985). Type of entrepreneur, type of firm, and managerial motivation: Implications for organizational life cycle theory, Strategic Management Journal.

Stogdill, R.M., & Coons, A.E. (1957). *Leader behavior: Its description and measurement*. Columbus, OH: Ohio State University Bureau of Business Research.Zaccaro, S.J., & Horn, Z.N. (2003). Leadership theory and practice: Fostering an effective symbiosis. The Leadership Quarterly, 14(6), 769-806.

Thompson, A. (2021). Kentucky colleges are going beyond teaching students the soft skills employers want Institutions are embedding these competencies into the curriculum and helping students learn how to talk about them. Higher Ed Dive.

Yukl, G. (2012). Effective leadership behavior: what we know and what questions need more attention. *Academy Of Management Perspectives*, 26(4), 66-85.

Zhu, W, Chew, IK & Spangler, WD 2005 CEO transformational leadership and organizational outcomes: The mediating role of human capital-enhancing human resource management, The Leadership Quarterly, vol. 16, no. 1, pp. 39-52.

Chapter 4

Avolio, BJ, Waldman, DA, and Yammarino, FJ 1991 'Leading in the 1990s: The Four I's of Transformational Leadership', *Journal of European Industrial Training*, vol. 15, no. 4, pp. 9-16.

Bloom, N., Genakos, C., Sadun, R., and Reenen, J. V. (2012). **Management Practices Across Firms and Countries**, Harvard Business School, Found on website on 5/31, 2021

https://www.hbs.edu/ris/Publication%20Files/Management_Practices_cd1ecd8a-6aeb-43e0-9d3d-f912ed242bf9.pdf

Chien, HJ 2001, *A comparison of leadership characteristics in public and large and small private organizations in Taiwan*, Nova Southeastern University.

Damanpour, F 1991 'Organizational innovation: A meta-analysis of effects of determinants and moderators', *Academy of Management Journal*, vol. 34, no. 3, pp. 555–590.

Dosik, D., Bhalla, V. & Bailey, A. (2020). A Lot Will Change—So Must Leadership, The BCG Henderson Institute is Boston Consulting Group's strategy think tank. **https://www.bcg.com/publications/2020/importance-of-transformative-leadership-post-coronavirus**

Jung, DI, Chow, C, and Wu, A 2003 'The role of transformational leadership in enhancing organizational innovation: Hypotheses and some preliminary findings', The Leadership Quarterly, vol. 14, no. 4–5, pp. 525-544.

Kasul, RA and Motwani, JG 1995 'Performance measurements in world class operations', *Benchmarking for Quality Management & Technology*, vol. 2, no. 2, pp. 20-36.

Management Matters in Australia: Just how productive are we? 2012, Department of Innovation, Industry, Science and Research, Australia.

Report of the Industry Task Force on Leadership and Management Skills 1995, Renewing Australian's managers to meet the challenges of the Asia-pacific century.

Chapter 5

Anderson, A & The American Productivity & Quality Centre 1996 The Knowledge Management Assessment Tool: External Benchmarking Version.

Burns, JM 1978, Leadership, Harper & Row, New York.

Frischer, J 2006 Laissez-faire Leadership versus Empowering Leadership in New Product Developing.

Hollander, EP 1984, Leadership Dynamics, Free Press, New York.

Jue, AL 2004 Towards a taxonomy of spirit-centered leadership as reflected in phenomenological experiences of entrepreneurial leaders.

Marturano, A & Gosling, J 2008, Leadership, Routledge, London.

Obiwuru, TC, Okwu, AT, Akpa, VO & Nwankwere, IA 2011 'Effects of leadership styles on organizational performance: A survey of selected small-scale enterprises in Ikosi-Ketu council development area of Lagos state', Australian Journal of Business and Management Research, vol. 1, no. 7, pp. 100-111.

Chapter 6

Adler, P.S, and Kwon, S. W. (2002). Social Capital: Prospects for a New Concept. The Academy of Management Review, 27(1), 17-40.

Bourdieu, P 1977 Outline of a theory of practice (tr. Richard Nice). Cambridge University Press, Cambridge.

Coleman, J.S 1988 Social Capital in the Creation of Human Capital. The American Journal of Sociology, 94(1), 95-120.

Putnam, R.D 1993 Making Democracy Work, Princeton, NJ: Princeton University Press.

Putnam, R.D 2000 Bowling alone: the collapse and revival of American community. New York: Simon & Schuster.

Schein, E. H. (2016). Organizational Culture and Leadership, Wiley; 5th edition.

Woolcock, M 1998 Social capital and economic development: toward a theoretical synthesis and policy framework, Theory and Society, 27(2), 151-208.

Chapter 7

Braga, D 2002 Transformational leadership attributes as perceived by team members of knowledge networks (Unpublished doctoral dissertation). Pepperdine University, USA.

Coakes E & Smith P 2007 Developing communities of innovation by identifying innovation champions. The Learning Organization, 14(1), 74 – 85.

Clawson, J. G. S. (2021). Fundamentals of Level Three Leadership: How to Become an Effective Executive. Business Expert Press, New York, New York.

Pemberton, J, Mavin, S & Stalker, B 2007 Scratching beneath the surface of communities of (mal)practice. Learning Organization, 14(1), 62–73.

Whyte, W. H. (2002). The Organizational Man, University of Pennsylvania Press

Chapter 8

Avila Cobo, S.H. (2005). Collaboration, innovation, and the building blocks of social capital in the technology sector: A comparative analysis of knowledge-creating institutions. The role of individual attributes, policies and environments in the collaboration and productivity of scientists and technologists, Thesis (PhD), Stanford University.

Choi, B. (2002) Knowledge Management Enablers, Processes, and Organizational Performance: An Integration and Empirical Examination, Thesis (PhD), Korea Advanced Institute of Science and Technology.

Coleman, J.S. (1988) Social Capital in the Creation of Human Capital, The American Journal of Sociology, vol. 94, no. 1, pp. 95-120.

Cots, E.G. (2011). Stakeholder social capital: a new approach to stakeholder theory, Business Ethics: A European Review, vol. 20, no. 4, pp. 328-341.

Daft, R.L. (1995). Organization theory and design, Minneapolis/St. Paul: West Pub. Co.

Nahapiet, J., and Ghoshal, S. (1998). Social Capital, Intellectual Capital, and the Organizational Advantage, The Academy of Management Review, vol. 23, no. 2, pp. 242-266.

Ostrom, E., & Ahn, T.K. (2003). Introduction. In Ostrom, E & Ahn, TK (ed.), Foundations of Social Capital, Cheltenham: Edward Elgar Publishing.

Putnam, R.D., Leonardi, R., & Nanetti, R. (1993). Making democracy work: civic traditions in modern Italy, Princeton: Princeton University Press.

Putnam, R.D. (2000) Bowling alone: the collapse and revival of American community, New York: Simon & Schuster.

Schein, E.H. (1985). Organizational culture and leadership, San Francisco: Jossey-Bass Publishers.

Wang, C.L. & Ahmed, P.K. (2003). Structure and structural dimensions for knowledge-based organizations, Measuring Business Excellence, vol. 7, no. 1, pp. 51-62.

Villalonga-Olives, E. & Kawachi, I. (2015) The measurement of social capital, Gaceta Sanitaria, vol. 29, no. 1, pp. 62-64.

Chapter 9

Andrews, K 1971, The Concept of Corporate Strategy, Irwin, Homewood, Illinois.

Ansoff, HI 1965, *Corporate strategy; an analytic approach to business policy for growth and expansion*, McGraw-Hill, NY.

Barclay's Insight (2020). "The Post-Covid Economy," found on website
https://www.investmentbank.barclays.com/our-insights/The-post-COVID-economy.html?cid=paidsearch-textads_google_google_themes_egs_post_covid_us_research_egs_post_covid_bmm_923227269019&gclid=Cj0KCQjwo-aCBhC-ARIsAAkNQitpCW_tYfqRW_QN6FFXX9sStbiJD2FYf8pVMKUggDoPFhsMHQgCqq8aAsDfEALw_wcB&gclsrc=aw.ds on 3,23,2021.

Barney, J. 1986 'Strategic factor markets: Expectations, luck, and business strategy', *Management Science*. vol. 32, no. 10, pp. 1231-1241.

Barney, J. (March 1991). "Firm Resources and Sustained Competitive Advantage". Journal of Management. 17 (1): 99–120.

Barney J 2002, *Gaining and Sustaining Competitive Advantage*, Prentice Hall, Upper Saddle River, NJ.

Conner, KR 1991 'A historical comparison of resource-based theory and five schools of thought within industrial economics: Do we have a new theory of the firm?' *Journal of Management*, vol. 17, no. 1, pp. 121-154.

Dierickx, I & Cool, K 1989 'Asset stock accumulation and sustainability of competitive advantage', *Management Science*. vol. 35, no. 12, pp. 1504-1511.

Grant, RM & Baden-Fuller, C 2004 'A knowledge accessing theory of strategic alliances', *Journal of Management Studies*, vol. 41, no. 1, pp. 619-652.

Hofer, CW & Schendel, D 1978, *Strategy Formulation: Analytical Concepts*. West Publishing Company, Saint Paul.

Hoskisson, RE, Hitt, MA, Wan, WP & Yiu, D 1999 'Swings of a pendulum: Theory and research in strategic management,' *Journal of Management*. Vol. 25, no. 3, pp. 417-456.

Hougaard, R., Carter, J., and Mohan, M. (March 2020)."Build Your Resilience in the Face of Crisis," *Harvard Business Review*.

Liebeskind, JP 1996 'Knowledge, strategy, and the theory of the firm', *Strategic Management Journal*, vol. 17, pp. 93-107.

Lippman, SA & Rumelt, RP 1982 'Uncertain imitability: Impediments to economic activity, market failures and profitability', *The Bell Journal of Economics*. vol. 13, pp. 418-438.

Penrose, ET 1959, *The theory of the growth of the firm*, Blackwell Oxford, GB.

Penrose, E 1980, *The Theory of the Growth of the firm*, 2nd edition, Basil Blackwell Publisher, Oxford.

Reus, TH 2004, *A knowledge-based view of international acquisition performance*, The Florida State University.

Teece, DJ 1986 'Profiting from technological innovation', *Research Policy*, vol. 15, pp. 285-305.

Wernerfelt, B 1984 'A Resource-based View of the Firm', *Strategic Management Journal* (pre-1986), vol. 5, no. 2, p. 171-180.

Zheng, W, Yang, B & Mclean, GN 2010 'Linking organizational culture, structure, strategy, and organizational effectiveness: Mediating role of knowledge management', *Journal of Business Research*, vol. 63, no. 7, pp. 763-771.

Chapter 10

Bayyavarapu, H.B. (2005). Knowledge management strategies and firm performance, Doctoral Dissertation, The University of Western Ontario, Canada.

Basel Committee on Banking Supervision (2020). Principles for operational resilience (**www.bis.org**). Found on website on 4, 7, 2021 **https://www.bis.org/bcbs/publ/d509.pdf**.

Crossan, M.M., Lane, H.W., & White, R.E. (1999). An Organizational Learning Framework: From Intuition to Institution. The Academy of Management Review, 24(3), 522-537.

Davenport, T.H., & Prusak, L. (1998). Working knowledge, Boston, MA: Harvard Business School Press.

Day, G. S., & Schoemaker, P. J. H. (2019). *See Sooner, Act Faster: How Vigilant Leaders Thrive in an Era of Digital Turbulence (Management on the Cutting Edge)*, The MIT Press.

Dorfler, V. (2010). Learning capability: the effect of existing knowledge on learning. Knowledge Management Research & Practice, 8, 369–379

Jones, K., & Leonard, L.K. (2009). From Tacit Knowledge to Organizational Knowledge for Successful KM. In W.R. King (Eds.), Knowledge Management and Organizational Learning, (pp. 27-39), Berlin: Springer.

Lau, A., & Tsui, E. (2009). Knowledge management perspective on e-learning effectiveness. Knowledge-Based Systems, 22(4), 324-325.

Linderman, K., Schoeder, R.G., Zaheer, S., Liedtke, C., & Choo, A.S. (2004). Integrating quality management practices with knowledge creation processes. Journal of Operations Management, 22(6), 589-607.

López, S.P., Peón, J.M.M., & Ordás, C.J.V. (2005). Organizational learning as a determining factor in business performance. The Learning Organization, 12(3), 227-245.

Matusik, S.F. (1998). The Utilization of Contingent Work, Knowledge Creation, and Competitive Advantage. The Academy of Management Review, 23(4), 680-697.

North K., Reinhardt, R., & Schmidt A. (2004). The Benefits of Knowledge Management: Some empirical evidence. v Retrieved from http://www2.warwick.ac.uk/fac/soc/wbs/rconf/olkc/archive /oklc5/papers/a-8_north.pdf.

Pandise, E. (2021). One Year Into Pandemic, Main Street Bankruptcies Continue. NBC News

Richmond, A. (2014). Should You (Ever) Go Over Your Boss's Head? Forbes Magazine. Found on 3,25,2021, at website **https://www.forbes.com/sites/85broads/2014/03/21/should-you-ever-go-over-your-bosss-head/?sh=75e62ec34bc9**.

Ruggles, RL 1997, Knowledge management tools, Boston, MA: Butterworth-Heinemann.

Sawhney, M. (2021). *Reimagining Executive Education*. Harvard Business Review (March 26).

Schoemaker, P. (2021). *4Sight Chat Ep. 9 – Paul Schoemaker: Vigilance, Foresight, and Business Schools*, Interview by Alex Fergnani. Found on website on March 3, 2021, **https://www.youtube.com/watch?v=DdtmJUPePNY&t=3s**

Sukumaran, S., Sukumaran, S., Shetty, M.V., & Shetty, M.V. (2009). Knowledge Management (KM) in automobile: Application of a value chain (VC) approach using KM tools, Retrieved from http://ieeexplore.ieee.org/stamp/stamp.jsp?arnumber=0 54025 54.

Templeton, G.F., Bruce, R.L., & Snyder, C.A. (2002). Development of a Measure for the Organizational Learning Construct. Journal of Management Information Systems, 19(2), 175-218.

Tsoukas, H. (1996). The Firm as a Distributed Knowledge System: A Constructionist Approach. Strategic Management Journal, 17, 11-25.

Vera, D., & Crossan M. (2003). Organizational Learning and Knowledge Management: Toward an Integrative Framework. In M. Easterby-Smith & M. Lyles (Eds.), Handbook of organizational learning and knowledge management, NJ: Wiley-Blackwell.

Wiig, K.M. (1994). Knowledge management foundations: Thinking about thinking- How people and organizations create, represent, and use knowledge. Arlington, Texas: Schema Press.

***

About the Authors

Michael J. Provitera is an executive leadership trainer. As president of Motivational Leadership Training, his focus is on improving organizational effectiveness and enhancing individual success. He has trained over 1000 executives. His executive leadership certification runs eighteen hours and covers six factors of leadership. A new specialized three-hour executive certification is now available. Clients have been Pfizer, Trane, Interval International, and the City of North Miami. Michael is sought by reporters for quotes in prominent media such as Forbes, US New & World Report, The Daily News, Fox Business, Higher Ed Jobs, Hr.Com, NBC News, and The Washington Times. The author can be contacted at: docprov@msn.com

Mostafa Sayyadi is an international management consultant. He works with senior business leaders to effectively develop innovation in companies and helps companies—from start-ups to the Fortune 100—succeed by improving the effectiveness of their leaders. He is a business book author and a long-time contributor to HR.com, Conscious Company Magazine, The Canadian Business Journal and Consulting Magazine and his work has been featured in these top-flight business publications. In recognition of his work with Australian Institute of Management and Australian Human Resources Institute, he has been awarded the titles, "Associate Fellow of the Australian Institute of Management" and "Senior Professional in Human Resources". The author can be contacted at: mostafasayyadi1@gmail. Com

www.ingramcontent.com/pod-product-compliance
Lightning Source LLC
Chambersburg PA
CBHW031625210526
45464CB00004B/1758